"Trust the past to the mercy of God, the present to
His love, and the future to His providence."

—St. Augustine

WHISTLE STOP Café MYSTERIES

For SENTIMENTAL REASONS

GABRIELLE MEYER

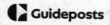

Guideposts

Whistle Stop Café Mysteries is a trademark of Guideposts.

Published by Guideposts
100 Reserve Road, Suite E200
Danbury, CT 06810
Guideposts.org

Cover and interior design by Müllerhaus
Cover illustration by Greg Copeland at Illustration Online LLC
Typeset by Aptara, Inc.

ISBN 978-1-961126-19-0 (hardcover)
ISBN 978-1-961126-20-6 (epub)

Printed and bound in the United States of America
10 9 8 7 6 5 4 3 2 1

For Sentimental Reasons

CHAPTER ONE

A cold wind rattled the windows on Debbie Albright's house as she pulled the pan of lasagna from her oven. The smell of basil and garlic wafted through her kitchen and made her stomach rumble. February in Ohio made her crave comfort foods, and she had spent much of the winter cooking some of her favorites. Since she lived alone, she knew she'd be eating lasagna for a few days. A thought that didn't bother her in the least.

The front doorbell rang, surprising her. She wasn't expecting anyone, although, since returning to her hometown of Dennison, she often had family and friends drop in.

She smiled to herself as she walked through her living room to the foyer. Things had changed since leaving her corporate job in Cleveland to come back to Dennison and open the Whistle Stop Café. She just wished she had made the move sooner. She loved impromptu visitors.

Debbie flipped on her front light and was surprised to see her aunt Sherry, her dad's sister. Aunt Sherry was almost eighty and didn't often go out in the evenings, especially during this time of year—and rarely by herself. In recent years, she'd been traveling to Arizona for the colder months. But this winter she had decided to stay in Dennison to get her house ready to sell. She planned to make a permanent move.

Debbie opened the door, allowing a gust of frosty air to blow past her.

"Come in," she said as she motioned for her aunt to enter. "It's cold out there."

Aunt Sherry held an old crate in her hands, making Debbie even more curious about her unexpected arrival.

"Hello, dear," Aunt Sherry said. "I hope I'm not bothering you."

"Of course not. I was just ready to sit down to eat supper. Would you like to join me?"

"Oh, I couldn't." Aunt Sherry wore a fur cap over her short gray hair. "I wouldn't want to bother you."

"You're no bother—and I have a whole pan of lasagna for myself. I'd love to share it."

"Well." Aunt Sherry glanced toward the kitchen and smiled. "I was just going to have a bowl of cereal when I got home."

"Then it's settled." Debbie took the crate from her aunt, surprised to see it filled with old baby items and a yellowed newspaper. "You're staying."

"It smells delicious." Aunt Sherry took off her heavy coat and her hat and set them on a hook.

"What did you bring for me?" Debbie asked as she indicated the crate.

Aunt Sherry's smile fell, and she shook her head. "I don't know what this is—that's why I brought it to you. I found it in the garage rafters today—or, I should say that my neighbor boy found it. I hired him to clean out the garage. You know I'm hoping to put my house up for sale soon, so I started going through things. And I found this crate."

Aunt Sherry had purchased her parents' house and had raised her two children there. Both of her kids had moved out of the area when Debbie was a little girl. Her husband had died a few years ago, and Aunt Sherry lived on her own.

"Let's take it into the living room," Debbie suggested. "The lasagna needs a few minutes to set before we cut into it."

Aunt Sherry followed Debbie, and they took a seat on the couch.

The crate was old and dusty. Cobwebs filled the corners, and the items within looked like they were in rough shape. There was a moth-eaten baby blanket, gray with age, though it must have been a soft pink at one time. There was also a silver rattle, a glass baby bottle, and a yellowed cotton sleeping gown.

"This is why I brought this stuff to you," Aunt Sherry said as she lifted the newspaper out of the crate. She carefully unfolded it and laid it on the coffee table.

"Look at the date," she said. "February fifteenth, 1944."

It was the Dennison newspaper, *The Evening Chronicle*. Right under the title of the paper was the biggest headline of the day. ALLIES ATTACK DURING STORM AND SHOVE GERMANS BACK IN BATTLE TO SAVE BEACHHEAD.

"This is interesting," Debbie said slowly. She didn't know why her aunt had brought it to her.

"Look at this." Aunt Sherry pointed to a smaller headline.

The ink was faded, so Debbie had to get closer to read it, but when she did, things started to make sense. "'Abandoned Baby Found at Dennison Depot by Depot Workers.'" Debbie went on to read the rest of the article out loud.

WHISTLE STOP CAFÉ MYSTERIES

"'A baby girl was found yesterday, February fourteenth, abandoned on the platform of the Dennison depot. The porter heard the baby crying after the last train pulled out, and located the child. It is believed the baby is only a few days old. She was in a wooden crate with nothing more than a pink blanket, a small silver rattle, an empty baby bottle, and the white cotton gown she wore. The police were called, and the baby was placed in the care of a Dennison family until the mother can be located. Please contact the Dennison Police Department if you have any information on the identity of the mother or if you saw anything suspicious at the depot yesterday.'"

Debbie met her aunt's concerned gaze.

"I thought," Aunt Sherry said, "that since you and Janet work at the depot and you've solved so many mysteries there, that you might be able to help me solve this one."

Debbie and her best friend, Janet Shaw, had opened the Whistle Stop Café at the depot the past summer, and Debbie had shared many stories with her aunt about the mysteries they had solved. She wasn't surprised that her aunt would think of her now.

"Have you heard about this baby before?" Aunt Sherry asked, her blue eyes searching Debbie's with surprising intensity.

"I haven't. I'm sorry. But I can see what Kim might know." Kim Smith was the director of the train museum, which was also housed in the depot. "I can ask some of my friends who worked at the depot and the Salvation Army canteen during the war. They might remember."

Aunt Sherry nodded and then gazed down at her hands.

"What's bothering you?" Debbie asked, putting her hand on her aunt's shoulder.

When Aunt Sherry finally looked up, she had tears in her eyes. "I was born on Valentine's Day in 1944, Debbie. My parents were married for a decade before I came along—and then it was many years after that before they had your father, and then, four years later, little Debra. Vance was a complete surprise. I remember when my mom got pregnant with him. I was twelve—almost thirteen—and it was the shock of her life. I vividly recall her saying, 'I never thought it was possible.'" Aunt Sherry shook her head. "At the time, I thought she said it because she was in her forties. But now, after finding this crate hidden in the garage and seeing the date on the newspaper, I can't help but wonder if she said it because she didn't think she could *ever* get pregnant. What if I'm the baby who was abandoned on the depot platform that day?"

Debbie stared at her aunt, speechless. She had never been led to believe that Aunt Sherry was adopted—but it was entirely possible. Debbie had inherited her father's brown eyes, and she'd been told that both of his parents had brown eyes. Yet Aunt Sherry had blue eyes. She was also taller than all the other women in her family and didn't look a thing like Debbie's father. Yet Debbie had never questioned any of this.

Until now.

"I'll be eighty years old two weeks from yesterday," Aunt Sherry continued, tears streaking down her wrinkled cheeks. "And suddenly my entire life feels like a lie."

Debbie reached out and took Aunt Sherry's hand in her own. "Even if it's true, your life is not a lie. You are Sherry Albright Hoffman. Your parents were Fred and Gertrude Albright, and your brother is Vance. You have led a happy, fulfilled life, and you have two wonderful children. None of that is a lie, Aunt Sherry."

"Why wouldn't my parents tell me the truth?" she asked.

"We don't even know if you are the baby from the depot."

"How will we find out?"

"We can look for some answers," Debbie said with confidence. "We'll first find out if the baby or her mother was ever identified. Perhaps she was returned to her mother. If nothing comes of that, and we still want to know, we can always have a DNA test done to see if you're related to my dad—or me."

"I don't think I'm quite ready for that yet. That's why I'd like you to find out what you can first. Because why would my parents have the crate and other things from this baby if it wasn't me?"

"I don't know. There has to be some good explanation. Maybe your parents were the ones who took care of the baby until she could be reunited with her mother, and they just never got around to getting these things to her." Debbie squeezed her aunt's hand. "There's always a logical reason. We just have to find it."

Aunt Sherry was quiet for a moment, and then she said, "If this is me—if I was the abandoned baby, I want to know who my birth mother is and why she left me on the depot platform."

Debbie studied her aunt. "Would you really want to know?"

"Yes." Aunt Sherry lifted her chin. "I'm almost eighty years old. I want to know for my children's and grandchildren's sake if nothing else. They should know their heritage."

"It's all conjecture at this point," Debbie said. "We don't even know if it's you. We'll cross that bridge when we get to it."

"Okay." Aunt Sherry wiped at her tears.

"Now," Debbie said as she stood, "how about we dig into that lasagna? It should be set and ready to eat."

"That sounds wonderful." Aunt Sherry smiled at Debbie. "And thanks for helping me."

"Of course. We'll find the answers, Aunt Sherry. Don't worry."

Debbie led Aunt Sherry into her kitchen, her mind churning with all the questions her aunt's discovery had created.

The morning sun had not yet peeked above the horizon the next day as Debbie left her house to go to the Whistle Stop Café. Janet did all the baking and arrived between four and five, but Debbie usually got there at six to open for their early-morning customers.

It was only a few blocks from Debbie's house to the depot where the café was located, and she often walked. But during the winter, when there was ice and snow on the ground, she almost always drove to work. Not only was it nice to have a warm vehicle, but it was also nice to have her car at work in case she needed to run errands after they closed the café.

This morning, Debbie was especially anxious to get to work to talk to Janet about what Aunt Sherry had found. Aunt Sherry had left the crate with Debbie, and Debbie had brought it with her to the café to show Janet.

She pulled up to the depot and parked her car. The air was brisk as she got out and grabbed the crate. It wasn't very big, and it was almost hard to imagine a newborn fitting inside. How desperate that mama must have felt to leave her baby on the depot platform, and how cold and alone the baby must have been. If the weather was anything like it was today, and all the baby had for protection was a blanket, it was a miracle she hadn't frozen to death.

Debbie had so many questions as she walked into the depot. They had been spinning in her mind since her aunt's visit and had caused her to dream some strange dreams. Who found the baby? Was the mother ever identified? Why did the mother abandon the baby? Did the birth father know? What happened to the baby?

Most importantly, *was* Aunt Sherry the baby?

Debbie unlocked the main doors of the depot and turned left. She flipped on a few lights and then walked through the original waiting area and past the ticket counter to get to the glass door that led into the café. That door was locked as well, since Janet usually entered the kitchen through the back door and left the main doors locked until Debbie arrived.

She loved the café. Loved being her own boss and working alongside her childhood friend. She especially loved the customers that came in every day. These were the regulars, but then there were visitors who came to Dennison to visit the museum or stay in the bed-and-breakfast train car behind the depot.

No matter why they came, Debbie relished being in the front of the café to visit and get to know people. Janet enjoyed that too, but she also loved being in the kitchen. They were a perfect team.

Only one light was on above the register, so Debbie turned the rest of them on and then walked across the room to set the crate on the long counter. Swivel stools lined the counter, while tables and chairs filled the rest of the room. Bright yellow walls were covered with vintage WWII posters that Debbie and Janet had collected, as well as old kitchen utensils and tools that Janet was given by her old employer. Behind the counter was a large chalkboard where they wrote the daily specials. Janet had already made the change from yesterday and had written *Meat loaf, mashed potatoes, gravy, and glazed carrots* for today's special.

Janet walked through the swinging door, pushing it open with her backside and bringing with her a sweet aroma. In her hands was a huge tray of caramel rolls, probably fresh out of the oven. Gooey, golden goodness oozed between the cracks and down the sides of the rolls.

"Oh boy," Debbie said, her stomach rumbling. "Those smell delicious."

"Hey." Janet smiled as she set the tray on the counter and opened the display case. She wore a pair of blue jeans and a graphic T-shirt, though Debbie couldn't read the words because her apron covered it.

"Good morning." Debbie slipped her coat off and hung it on the hook near the kitchen door. She took her apron from the hook next to it, put it on, and tied the strings.

"What's this?" Janet asked as she wiped her hands on her apron and nodded at the crate.

Debbie walked to the counter, adjusting her apron to fit over her blouse and blue jeans. "My aunt Sherry brought this to me last night."

"It looks old."

"The newspaper is from February fifteenth, 1944."

Janet lifted her eyebrows. Her chin-length blond hair was tucked behind her ears, and her hazel eyes were filled with curiosity. "What's up with the baby stuff?"

"Read the article at the bottom of the front page."

As Janet pulled the paper out and started reading the article, Debbie walked behind the counter and grabbed a plate and a mug. The smell of coffee already permeated the air, since Janet often started the first pot when she came in. Debbie filled her mug and helped herself to one of the caramel rolls.

"Wow," Janet said. "I've never heard about this. Have you?"

"No." Debbie took a seat on one of the stools and sipped the coffee, savoring the flavor and warmth. "But my aunt is concerned. She was born on February fourteenth, 1944, and she found the crate and the items inside the garage that used to belong to her parents. She thinks she might be the baby."

Janet frowned. "Did her parents ever say anything about adopting her?"

"Never." Debbie realized she had forgotten a fork, but Janet came to her rescue and handed her one. "Thanks."

Debbie cut into the caramel roll. It was so soft and moist, her mouth started to water even before she tasted it. "My grandparents were married for over ten years before my aunt was born, and then they didn't have my dad for another thirteen years. Aunt Sherry said that her mother claimed she never thought it was possible to get pregnant when she found out she was having Dad."

"Well, that's strange."

"I thought the same thing. My aunt is pretty shaken up about it." Debbie took the first bite, and it practically melted in her mouth. "This is really good, Janet."

"Thanks." Janet smiled, but then she nodded at the crate. "What do you think? Is it possible your aunt is the baby who was abandoned on the depot platform?"

"I don't know, but I can't rule it out."

"I wonder if Eileen remembers what happened."

"That's what I was wondering too."

Eileen Palmer was the stationmaster at the Dennison depot during the war years, when the Salvation Army canteen served over a million soldiers as they came through town. She now lived at the Good Shepherd Retirement Center and had a wealth of knowledge about the town. She was also Kim Smith's mother.

"Kim might know something too," Janet said. "We should ask her."

Debbie nodded. "Are you free to run out to Good Shepherd with me after we close? I'll call Eileen and see if she's able to visit with us."

"I think that should work."

"Great."

A timer went off in the kitchen. "Those are my cranberry muffins," Janet said, and hurried off.

Debbie quickly finished her caramel roll as the first customer, Patricia Franklin, entered the café.

"Morning," Debbie said to Patricia.

"Good morning." Patricia shivered and then said, "Brr. It's cold out there today."

"I'm ready for a warm-up."

"Me too."

"The usual?"

"You know it."

Debbie took another sip of coffee and picked up her dirty plate to put it in the bin under the counter. She kept her coffee close at hand as she made a peppermint mocha for Patricia. "Janet has some fresh caramel rolls—"

"No need to convince me." Patricia grinned as she came over to the counter. "Sounds wonderful."

The day had begun, and Debbie was off and running, but she couldn't stop thinking about her aunt Sherry or the crate of baby items. As soon as she finished making Patricia's coffee, she lifted the crate off the counter and set it in the back, near the door that led outside.

More than anything, she hoped her aunt would get an answer that made her happy. But if she didn't, Debbie prayed that they could identify the birth mother and get the answers they needed.

CHAPTER TWO

A light snow fell from the heavy clouds overhead as Debbie sat in the passenger seat of Janet's car. Up ahead, the Good Shepherd Retirement Center was situated on a slight hill with tall pine trees all around. It felt almost like home to Debbie, since her father used to be the director of the facility before he retired. She had spent many hours of her childhood with the residents of Good Shepherd and continued to visit her friends who lived there now.

"The forecast is calling for four inches of snow tonight," Janet said as she looked up at the sky. "I'm ready for spring."

"You and me both." Debbie's phone began to vibrate in her purse, near her feet. She reached down and took the phone out, reading the name GREG CONNOR on the screen.

Janet glanced over and smiled at Debbie. "Gonna answer that?"

"Of course I am." Debbie and Greg met when Debbie moved back to Dennison. They had both grown up in town, but Greg was a few years older, and they hadn't gone through school together. His wife had died a few years ago, leaving him with two teenage boys, Jaxon and Julian. He attended the same church Debbie did and had done some construction work at her house. Their friendship had grown over the months, but with his two sons and running his own construction company, Greg had a lot on his plate.

Debbie pressed the green icon and put the phone to her ear. "Hello?"

"Hey, Debbie, it's Greg."

"Hi, Greg." Her cheeks felt warm at his unexpected call. "What can I do for you?"

"I'm sorry to bother you, and I wish I could have prepared my speech a little more, but the truth is, I'm in sort of a pickle and wondering if you could help me out."

"What's the trouble?"

"Well, you know I'm on the board of directors for the Homes for Humanity organization in town. We always hold our annual fundraiser in mid-February. It's one of the most important events of our year and makes up a big portion of our budget."

"I've always admired that organization," Debbie said. "I had a friend in Cleveland who lost her house in a fire, and Homes for Humanity volunteers built her a new one."

"I'm glad to hear it. We survive through donations and fundraisers, which is why our February fundraiser is so important."

"What can I do to help?" Debbie already knew she'd do what she could, no matter what Greg asked. Not only was the organization a worthy cause, but he had a need, and she believed firmly in supporting friends.

"At our last meeting, we learned our fundraiser planner hasn't been doing his job—to state it simply. There's only two weeks left until the event, and he hasn't solidified any plans, so we've asked him to step down from the board. I know it's a lot to ask, but I'm wondering if you'd consider attending a meeting tonight to help us come up with a new plan and then implement it. This is going to be a lot of work, so if you'd rather not—"

"I'll be there, Greg."

She could hear the relief in his sigh. "Thank you, Debbie. This means a lot to me. Can I pick you up about a quarter to seven for the meeting?"

"Sure."

"Great. Thanks. I'll see you then."

"You're welcome. See you tonight." Debbie ended the call.

Janet glanced at her as they pulled into the parking lot at Good Shepherd. "What was that about?"

"Greg's desperate for some help with a Homes for Humanity fundraiser."

"He was smart to call you. You're the best volunteer in Dennison."

Debbie smiled. "Second only to you."

They got out of the car and headed into the retirement home. Snowflakes fell on Debbie's face, melting on contact as she carried Aunt Sherry's crate. One of the maintenance guys was outside with a broom, sweeping off the front walk to keep the snow from piling up.

"Good afternoon," he said, nodding at them.

Debbie said hello as they walked past him and entered the warm building. They stopped at the front desk to check in and then headed toward Eileen's room, greeting familiar staff members as they walked down the hallway.

"Is Eileen expecting us?" Janet asked.

"I called her earlier today," Debbie assured her friend. "She said she was free all afternoon."

Debbie knocked on Eileen's door, which was ajar. "Hello," she called. "Anyone home?"

"Come on in, honey," Eileen said. "We're just enjoying a cup of coffee and some cookies."

Debbie pushed the door open and smiled when she saw Ray Zink sitting in his wheelchair across the table from Eileen. The two had known each other their entire lives and had become almost inseparable after Debbie and Janet had helped Ray find his long-lost love, Eleanor, and put an old romance to rest. Since then, he'd been spending more and more time with Eileen, and Debbie often wondered if the two were sweet on each other.

"Hello," Ray said, grinning. He was in his upper nineties and had lived most of his life in the house that Debbie now owned. It was because of him that she had been able to move back to Dennison with little trouble. The house was built by Ray's father, and Debbie was just the third owner since 1927. It was something she still marveled at, and it made her want to be extra mindful of taking care of the beautiful bungalow.

"I had the staff leave extra coffee and cookies, since I knew you were coming," Eileen said. "Pull up a chair and join us."

Debbie set the crate on a side table and then took a seat. The four of them drank their coffee and made small talk about the weather and the café and life at the retirement home.

When Debbie reached for her third cookie, Eileen said, "Now, tell us what brings you two here." She had a glimmer of interest in her eyes, and Debbie presumed she'd guessed they'd come to ask her about another mystery from the past. Eileen loved to talk about her years working at the Dennison depot.

Debbie stood and fetched the crate. She brought it back to the table, where Janet made room.

"My aunt, Sherry Hoffman, found this in her garage rafters a couple of days ago. She brought it to me with lots of questions." Debbie was eager to hear what Eileen might remember from February 1944. Ray would have been serving overseas at that point, but he still heard a lot of stories about what had happened in Dennison when he returned. He might know something too.

Eileen lifted the sleeping gown with gentle hands. Her fingers were thin and gnarled, with dark blue veins under the translucent skin. They were hands that had served her and others well.

She frowned when she held the tarnished silver rattle and then the glass bottle. She set them aside and picked up the delicate blanket. It was filled with so many moth-eaten holes, it looked like it could fall apart if a gust of wind blew through the room. But it was the newspaper that made Eileen's eyes light up with recognition.

"My goodness," she said, almost to herself. "To see this after all these years…"

"What is it?" Ray asked her.

"Baby Sarah," Eileen said. "At least, that's what we called her. I was working that day." She paused and shook her head. "She was so small— no more than a few days old. The umbilical cord hadn't been properly taken care of. It was clear that there was no doctor at the birth. Whoever left the baby on the platform had to have been panicked."

"They never found the mother?" Debbie asked.

"No." Eileen shook her head again as she gazed at the newspaper. "We looked for months—the police were involved and everything—but the mother never came forward, and we didn't have enough clues to find her. Besides, there was a war on, and there weren't enough officers to put on the case."

"What happened to the baby?" Janet asked.

Eileen frowned as she set the newspaper down. "I was never told. The family who adopted her wanted to remain anonymous. I took care of her for several weeks until a social worker from New Philadelphia found a permanent home for her. I worked with the police to locate the mother, but it came to nothing."

Ray picked up the rattle. "Did you have any leads?" he asked.

"A few women became prime suspects." Eileen waved her hand. "But we couldn't find conclusive evidence and, eventually, we stopped looking. I even remember getting on a train and going to another town—" She paused. "Or did I go by car? Either way, I tried to find the mother, but nothing ever came of my efforts."

"Do you think you could help me find her now?" Debbie asked.

Eileen frowned. "If I couldn't find her eighty years ago, what makes you think we could find her today?"

"I don't know," Debbie admitted. "But I want to try."

"I'm happy to tell you what I remember," Eileen said, "but I can't see how that will help you."

Debbie smiled. "I'll take whatever you can remember."

Eileen leaned back in her chair. "What I remember most about that day was how cold it was...."

February 14, 1944

"Won't it ever get warm again, Miss Eileen?" Harry Franklin asked as he blew into the lobby, holding his hat on his head so it wouldn't go flying. Snow followed him in, along with the howling of the wind. He shoved the door closed. "The thermometer read minus five this morning, and I don't think it's gotten much warmer. If it doesn't stop snowing, I don't know how the trains will get through."

Eileen stood behind the ticket counter in the cold lobby, a clipboard in hand as she looked over the day's schedule. The last train had just pulled out seconds ago, and she expected a troop train in about an hour. The Salvation Army canteen workers on duty would need to be informed. There would be coffee to make, sandwiches to assemble, and cookies to wrap. The service members would only have about twenty minutes to eat and enjoy their coffee while the train was being refueled, and in that time, the volunteers would serve hundreds of them. They would also provide reading material and playing cards, conversation, and hope. The service members had dubbed

Dennison "Dreamville, Ohio" because of the canteen, and Eileen took great pride in running the station that brought so much happiness.

"It should start warming up sooner rather than later," Eileen reassured Harry as she hung the clipboard on the wall behind the ticket counter. "It can't stay winter forever."

Harry was only fifteen, but he had grown up a lot since he'd started working at the depot. He shook his head, his brown eyes weary. "Sometimes it feels like it'll never be spring again."

Eileen put her hand on his shoulder. "I know what you mean, Harry, but this can't last forever."

They both knew she was talking about the war as well as the winter. The conflict had dragged on for over two years now, and it didn't look like there was an end in sight. Eileen had to keep hope alive though, and it was her job to pass that hope along to everyone she encountered.

"I'll head on out and clear the platform," Harry said. "We don't want our service members to climb over piles of snow to get their coffee."

"And I'll let the canteen workers know to expect a troop train within the hour." Eileen left Harry and walked toward the old café, where the canteen workers had set up their assembly line.

A young woman pulled the main doors open and entered the depot with a gust of wind. She shook the snow from her shoulders as she looked anxiously around the lobby.

"Abigail!" Eileen said with a smile. "I almost didn't recognize you. Welcome back to Dennison."

Abigail Cobb was only in her late teens, but she looked older and more careworn than the last time Eileen had seen her. Her cheeks were pale, and her eyes had dark shadows underneath them. She wore a faded blue coat and a simple black hat.

"Hello, Miss Eileen."

"It's good to see you again. How long has it been since you've been to the canteen?" Eileen tried to keep her voice light and unconcerned. Hundreds of volunteers came to the canteen to help. Some, like the local girls or those who had friends in Dennison or boarded nearby, showed up every day. Others drove into Dennison from neighboring towns on a rotating schedule to take their turns. Abigail was a local girl.

"It's been six months," Abigail said. "I just got back and wanted to come help." She looked toward the platform doors, as if searching for someone or something.

"It's good to have you." Eileen smiled. "Why don't you get yourself a sandwich and have a cup of coffee to warm up? The next troop train will be here soon, and then we'll all be busy."

Abigail followed Eileen to the café.

It was bustling inside as dozens of women from New Philadelphia visited and gossiped while making sandwiches. The smell of coffee and fresh-baked cookies filled the air.

Eileen showed Abigail where she could get a sandwich, and then she clapped her hands to get everyone's attention.

The room quieted, and Eileen caught the eye of familiar volunteers, as well as a couple of new ones she hadn't seen before.

"The next troop train will be here in less than an hour," she said. "Columbus wired and said there are four hundred and fifty soldiers coming our way."

A buzzing noise filled the room again as the women scurried to get everything ready.

Harry entered the café, his eyes wild as he looked around the room. When his gaze landed on Eileen, he motioned for her to join him.

Eileen's pulse jumped at the expression on Harry's face. He was usually so calm and unhurried—but something had him visibly shaken.

"What is it, Harry?" Eileen asked as she followed him out into the empty lobby.

"When I was clearing the snow, I heard something strange on the platform, like a kitten mewing or something." He hurried toward the ticket counter, so Eileen followed him. A wooden box sat on the counter. "Then I saw this crate. I thought I was going to find a litter of abandoned kittens in it—but look."

Eileen peeked over the edge of the crate, and her breath caught in her throat.

A tiny baby lay within, wrapped in a light pink blanket. It had a mass of dark hair that looked strange against the blue skin.

"What in the world?" Eileen reached and lifted the baby—a girl, guessing from the blanket—out of the crate.

The baby began to cry, but the noise she made was so weak, it was a wonder that Harry had heard it over the storm outside. The baby tried to nuzzle against Eileen but didn't have much strength.

"We need to get her warm," Eileen said. "There are some blankets in the storage room—run, Harry!"

He darted off.

"Who are you, little one?" Eileen whispered as she touched the baby's cheek. She was so tiny—so *defenseless. Who would have left her out in such horrible weather?*

She unwrapped the blanket and saw that the baby had on a soiled diaper and an old cotton sleeper. She lifted the sleeper and saw that whoever had given birth to the baby had not had medical help. Thankfully, they had known enough to tie off the umbilical cord with string, but it was not done well.

"You need a doctor and food," Eileen said as she wrapped the baby up again and held her close for warmth. She remembered that one of the volunteers who had come in from New Philadelphia had brought a baby with her. Perhaps she could be helpful while they waited for the doctor and the police.

But Eileen didn't want to create a stir moments before the troop train arrived, so she waited for Harry, who returned with a blanket in record time. As Eileen wrapped the baby in the second blanket, she asked him to locate Mrs. Jefferson.

The baby fussed again, this time a little harder.

Finally, Mrs. Jefferson appeared with Harry. She had a curious look on her face as she approached Eileen.

"Can I help you?" she asked.

"Our station porter just found this baby abandoned on the platform." Eileen pulled the blanket back
to show Mrs. Jefferson. "There's a bottle in the crate
that's empty, but she's hungry. Can you help while
I call the police and the doctor?"

Mrs. Jefferson's face revealed her shock and
concern as she nodded. "I'd be happy to help." She took
the baby into her arms, and Eileen led her into her
office. She made sure Mrs. Jefferson was settled and
comfortable and then closed the door to give her pri-
vacy to nurse the baby.

"Go finish shoveling the platform," Eileen said
to Harry. "We need to act like nothing has happened
until the police get here. I don't want to cause a scene."

"Yes, ma'am," Harry said as he started to head
outside.

Eileen touched his arm. "Thank you, Harry. You
saved that baby's life."

Harry lifted his chin and left the depot to finish
his job.

Eileen went to the telephone behind the ticket
counter and called the police. They would need to work
fast to locate the mother. If she had come by train, she
couldn't have gotten far. The last train had left just
minutes ago. If she had come by foot, she had to be close.

"Dennison Police Department," a man said when he answered.

"Hi, Officer Forest, this is Eileen Turner at the depot," she said. "I need someone to come as quickly as they can. A baby was abandoned on the platform, and we found it about five minutes ago. It can't be more than a few days old, if that."

"A baby?" Charles Forest was one of the day policemen. He often helped at the depot when a police presence was needed. "I'll be there as soon as I can."

"Thank you." Eileen hung up and then called Dr. Powers. He was an older man who had taken care of most of Dennison and the surrounding communities for as long as Eileen could remember. She prayed he'd be at home.

"Hello?" came a woman's voice.

"Mrs. Powers, this is Eileen Turner at the depot. Is Dr. Powers available to come here to examine a newborn baby?"

"He's just finishing his lunch, dear," Mrs. Powers said. "I'll send him over when he's done."

"The baby was abandoned on the platform in this cold weather with only a cotton gown and a thin blanket. If Dr. Powers could come as soon as possible, I'd appreciate it."

"Oh my," Mrs. Powers said. "I'll send him right over."

"Thank you." Eileen hung up and walked into her office to check on Mrs. Jefferson. "Is she eating?"

"It took her a little bit to get the hang of it," Mrs. Jefferson said, "but she's filling her tummy now."

Eileen smiled. "Thank you so much for being willing to do this."

"Of course. I'm happy to help. Do you know who left this sweet baby out there?"

"I have no idea, but I don't think they could have gotten very far. I hope the police can find the mother. She probably needs help too."

Mrs. Jefferson leaned forward. "There are a couple of new gals who just arrived at the canteen today. One of them is an Amish girl, Rebekah, I believe she said her name was. She's quiet and has kept to herself. The other one is a farm girl, Polly Pinehurst. I've seen her before, helping her father haul supplies into town. Both girls showed up sudden-like, and they're asking if there's somewhere for them to stay. We told them about the Snodgrass house, since Mrs. Snodgrass has been keen on taking in boarders in the past."

Eileen thought about Abigail, who had just shown up that day as well. Could one of them be the mother of the baby?

"Thank you for your help," Eileen said. "I know Polly. I'll be sure to ask her and Rebekah, and I'll have the police question them—and anyone else that appears suspicious." Abigail would be on that list too.

The mother had to be somewhere close, and Eileen was determined to find her.

CHAPTER THREE

*L*ater that evening, Debbie sat at her kitchen table and ate a piece of the leftover lasagna, thinking about her visit to Good Shepherd with Janet. Eileen had been helpful in describing the events that had happened the day the baby was discovered. She said she hadn't thought about it in years and would try to recall other details that Debbie might find useful.

Debbie glanced at the clock. It was six thirty, and she expected Greg to be there soon to pick her up. She quickly finished her supper and washed the dishes. After putting them away, she went upstairs to her room and changed into a fresh outfit. She didn't want to over-dress for the meeting, but she didn't want to wear the clothes she'd had on at the café either.

After putting on a pair of black jeans and a charcoal-gray blouse, she went into the bathroom and brushed her teeth and ran a comb through her hair. She put on a little lipstick and then went back to her room to slip on her black ankle boots. It was still snowing, and she wasn't sure if the sidewalks would be clear. Any extra protection against the cold and wet would be helpful.

The doorbell rang a few minutes later. Debbie flipped off her bedroom light and went downstairs, opened the door, and found

Greg standing on her covered porch in a wool coat with a cap over his dark hair.

"Hello," he said. Dimples appeared in his cheeks, reminding Debbie how much she liked seeing him smile.

"Hi." She motioned for him to come inside. "Stay warm while I get my coat."

He stepped into the house and closed the front door. "It smells great in here."

"Just leftover lasagna for supper." She opened the front closet and grabbed her coat and purse.

"Thanks again for agreeing to help out with the fundraiser," he said as he helped her with her coat. "I know I'm asking a lot—and I don't even know the full extent of our needs yet. Because it's an annual event, everyone knows when it will be, but we haven't announced what it is yet. Brian said he had everything under control, but we don't know what he was planning or if he made any progress on the plans. What we do know is that we have to hold the event in two weeks, because it's always the Saturday closest to Valentine's Day."

"I'm happy to lend a hand." Debbie buttoned up her coat. "I enjoy being involved in community events."

Greg's dimples made another appearance. "That's one of the reasons you came to mind."

Debbie almost said that she was happy to do anything that gave her an excuse to spend more time in his company, but she didn't want to say something that could make both of them uncomfortable. No matter how true it might be.

"We should probably get going," she said instead. "How are the roads?"

"They're a mess, but the snowplows are out, so that should help."

Debbie flipped the entry light off as Greg stepped out onto the porch. After locking the door, she followed him to his truck. Even though it was dark, she could see the Connor Construction logo on the side.

The snow fell heavier now than it had that afternoon. Debbie looked up into the dark sky, marveling at the beauty of it. Large snowflakes fell from the impossibly black sky, as if appearing out of nowhere.

Greg turned around on the sidewalk and grinned at her. "The winter gets long, but I never get tired of watching the snow fall."

Debbie smiled back at him. "It's almost magical, isn't it?"

They got into Greg's truck and drove to the Homes for Humanity office, which was housed in a storefront building in downtown Dennison. The lights were on, and Debbie could see a group of people sitting at a table behind the plate-glass windows.

"Marnie Hoskins is the executive director of our local HOH chapter," Greg explained as he parked his truck. "There are ten members on the board of directors, two paid and eight volunteer. I'm currently the president."

"Wow," Debbie said as she unbuckled her seat belt. "I didn't realize there were so many people involved."

"Well, we're down one board member now," Greg said. "As I mentioned, we dismissed Brian after we learned he dropped the ball on this event. But we're very fortunate to have such a strong board."

They got out and walked toward the building. They weren't far from the depot, which was the center of town. Snowflakes fell in a gentle cadence, reflected in the streetlights up and down Main Street.

Greg opened the door for Debbie, and they walked in together.

It was warm inside the building and smelled like freshly brewed coffee.

"Hello, Greg," said a woman from the head of the table. "You're just in time."

"Hello, Marnie," Greg said as he took off his cap and motioned to Debbie. "This is Debbie Albright. She's agreed to step in and help us with the fundraiser."

Marnie stood and extended her hand to Debbie, but her smile felt a little cool. She appeared to be in her late thirties and was well-dressed, carrying herself with a professional demeanor. Her dark brown hair was pulled back in a bun, and she wore a blazer and slacks. She seemed to assess Debbie as they shook hands, as if sizing her up. "It's nice to meet you," Marnie said. "Thank you for your willingness to pitch in. I tried to convince Greg that I didn't need more help, but he said I shouldn't have to do it all alone." She smiled at Greg, her cheeks turning pink. "He's always so thoughtful."

Debbie slipped off her coat. Greg took it from her and hung it on the coatrack next to his.

"Thank you," Debbie said.

"My pleasure."

Marnie went back to her spot at the table, and Debbie took a seat in one of the empty chairs. Greg sat down beside her, but Marnie said, "Greg, I saved you a spot next to me."

Greg glanced from Debbie to Marnie and hesitated for a second.

"You're the president of the board," Marnie said. "You should be here at the head of the table."

"Sorry," Greg said to Debbie.

"It's okay," she assured him as he picked up his folder and moved to the spot next to Marnie.

After Greg called the meeting to order, everyone introduced themselves. Seven board members were present, including Marnie and her executive assistant, Lexi. When the introductions were over, the secretary went through the minutes of the last meeting and the treasurer gave his report.

When it was time to discuss new business, Greg cleared his throat. "As many of you know, our fundraiser is just two weeks away," he said. "And it's come to our attention that very little has been planned. We're basically starting from scratch. We'll not only need to plan the entire event, but we'll need to make some basic decisions tonight so we can alter the advertising and marketing that's been done. We want to make sure we have as many people attend as possible." He glanced around the table, his gaze landing on Debbie. "I've asked Debbie to help us plan the event, and she's agreed. So, Debbie, if you have any ideas, we'd love to hear them. We're open to all suggestions."

"I think we should do what we do every year," Marnie said. "A chili dinner always goes over well in February. We can hold it at the community church. No need to start from scratch or do something different."

"While I appreciate the idea," Greg said, "Brian burned too many bridges at the church. I think we need to shake things up. Our attendance numbers have been falling steadily through the years, and I think people are getting bored with the chili dinner. I was thinking it would be fun to have something altogether different— maybe something like a dance."

Debbie immediately thought of the dances at the Dennison train station during the war. Eileen had told her all about them.

"There used to be dances at the depot," she said. "During the war years, when the Salvation Army canteen operated, they would hold a dance every week to raise funds. Do you think the depot lobby is big enough to accommodate the number of people who come to your fundraiser?"

Greg's eyes lit up. "I think it is," he said. "I like that idea. We could even give it a forties theme. Have a live band come in to play and advertise it as a swing dance."

"And we could serve a meal they would have served during the canteen days," Debbie said, her excitement growing. "It wouldn't be fancy, but it would be easy to serve and eat during a dance. We could elaborate on it a little, since they only served sandwiches, a cookie or donut, and coffee. I can talk to Janet to see if the café could possibly cater the event. We could include chips, a fruit salad, and a potato or pasta salad."

"Well," Marnie said, lifting her chin, "as nice as that sounds, I wouldn't want anyone to think that you joined the committee to benefit your own business."

Debbie frowned. "I didn't mean—"

"Of course you didn't," Greg said, frowning at Marnie. "I was the one who invited Debbie to help. She isn't doing this to benefit herself or her business."

"I'm happy to donate my time," Debbie said, her cheeks warm from Marnie's accusation, "if the board is willing to pay for the supplies. I'm sure Janet would be willing to do the same."

"That won't be necessary," Greg assured her. "The board can pay for your time preparing a meal."

"I like this idea," said one of the other board members. "It's unique and special for Dennison, given our history with the depot and the Salvation Army canteen."

"I agree," said another. "I wasn't excited about another chili dinner, but I'd love to attend a WWII-era dance at the depot. That sounds like a lot of fun. I think others would like it too."

Everyone but Marnie nodded their approval.

"I think it's a brilliant idea," Greg said. "I can look for a band. I remember hearing about one in Uhrichsville that plays big-band-era music. I don't know if they're free that weekend, but it would be worth checking into."

"We should promote it as a Valentine's Day dance," Debbie added. "It'll fall a couple days after Valentine's Day, but I think people will still be looking for something fun to do to celebrate the holiday."

"That's a great idea," said Lexi. "I was just talking to my husband the other day about what we're going to do for Valentine's Day. I'll tell him I have a plan now. He'll be happy he doesn't have to make reservations at a crowded restaurant."

"Then it's settled," Greg said. "We'll host a Valentine's Day dance and canteen dinner at the depot. Does anyone oppose this idea?"

"I don't think it's a smart move," Marnie said, leaning back and crossing her arms. "People are going to expect the chili dinner. But I can see I'm outnumbered, so I'll go along with what everyone else decides to do."

"Wonderful." Greg smiled at Debbie. "Thank you for your ideas."

Debbie couldn't hide her excitement, but then she remembered something important. "I don't know how to swing dance."

"You'll have time to learn," Greg said with a grin.

"In two weeks?" Marnie snorted. "I doubt it's possible. Especially if Debbie is going to pull off this event. She'll need to put all her spare time into it."

"Nothing is impossible," Greg said. "Who knows what can happen in two weeks?"

Debbie returned his smile, happy he had asked her to help. And even more excited to work on a project with him.

Despite Marnie Hoskin's negative attitude.

The snow was coming down harder as Greg drove Debbie home after the meeting. It had gathered on the roads and sidewalks, on houses and tree branches, and covered the yards.

"It looks like a winter wonderland," Debbie mused as Greg turned onto her street. "Even if it's cold, it sure is beautiful, isn't it?"

"I actually like winter." Greg drove slowly, so he wouldn't spin on the slippery roads. "Each season has a beauty all its own. I'm reminded how fast each one passes when I look at my boys. I don't like to wish time away. I try to appreciate each season I'm in."

"I like that perspective." Debbie hugged herself, trying to warm up. "But I still like summer better."

Greg laughed. "Me too."

He pulled into her driveway and put the truck into park.

Debbie wasn't sure if she should invite him in for coffee. It was getting late, and he'd probably want to get home to his boys.

"Thank you for coming, Debbie. I know Marnie can be a little... difficult sometimes." He said the words carefully. "She means well and is passionate about the organization. She moved here from California to take this job last year and is still working hard to fit in and prove herself. I think she feels out of her element in a small town. She doesn't have the same kind of connections that we locals have."

It sounded to Debbie like Greg was trying to make excuses for Marnie's behavior during the meeting. Marnie had made it clear she didn't like Debbie's ideas but was playing nice because she was out-voted. Why was he trying so hard to get Debbie to like Marnie? Was it so Debbie would keep working on the project? Or did he see something in the abrasive woman that Debbie didn't see? Did he have feelings for her?

"I can appreciate her struggle," Debbie said. "I had a hard time finding my way in Cleveland when I first moved there. It was such a big city, and I was used to a small town. It took me a long time to make friends and feel like I was part of a community at work and in my neighborhood."

"I suppose people struggle, no matter where they move," Greg said. "If they go from a small town to a big city, or a big city to a small town. I just hope she doesn't turn you off to helping us."

"It's okay," Debbie said. "I can handle it."

Greg smiled. "I know you can."

"Good." The truck was starting to warm up, and Debbie didn't want to leave Greg's company, but it was getting late, and she needed to be at the café early in the morning. "It was nice to see you again."

"You too."

"I'll talk to Janet about catering the event and reserve the depot lobby for the dance. I'll text you when I have those things lined up."

"And I'll check into the band in Uhrichsville tomorrow and let you know what I find out."

"Perfect. Call me if you need me."

"I will. Good night, Debbie."

"Good night, Greg." She opened the door and stepped gingerly through the snow to her front door.

"Do you need someone to shovel your driveway and sidewalks?" Greg called.

Debbie turned and saw that he had rolled down the window to talk to her.

"No, thanks. I have a neighbor boy who comes by before he leaves for school in the morning. It's a nice little side job for him."

"Okay." Greg waved and rolled up the window, but he didn't pull out of her driveway until she was safely inside the house.

Debbie stood in her foyer and watched his truck lights as he backed out and turned onto the street.

After she took off her coat and hung it in the closet with her purse, she sighed with happiness. Whenever she spent time with Greg, she felt peaceful and content in a way she hadn't since she'd been with her late fiancé, Reed. She had stayed in Cleveland after college to be near him, but he was deployed to Afghanistan, taken hostage, and then came word that he'd been killed. It had taken her years to come to terms with the loss of her dreams.

For the first time since Reed's death, Debbie had found a man who made her sit up and take notice again. Greg Connor was a truly good person. Even before she'd met him, she'd heard only positive and shining reports from everyone who said his name.

Debbie now knew why.

She walked up the steps, more aware of the solitude of her house than ever before—the creaking stairs, the howling wind, the empty rooms. She'd lived alone all her adult life, but there were times she felt more alone than others. And tonight, with the snow falling and the glow of Greg's company still filling her with warmth, she longed for a companion. Someone to discuss the day, to share both her joys and sorrows, her hopes and dreams and regrets.

Debbie flipped on her bedroom light and decided to stop focusing on what she didn't have and instead thank God for what she did have. Her snug home, her successful business, her good friends, and her loving family.

Thinking of her family made her remember her promise to Aunt Sherry to look for the truth about the abandoned baby. Tomorrow, when she spoke to Kim about the possible WWII-era dance at the depot, she'd also ask her what she knew about the child.

If it turned out that Sherry *was* the baby from the depot, it would answer one question but pose several more. Questions Debbie wasn't sure they could find answers for.

But she wouldn't give up. She'd solved harder mysteries in the past, and she could do it again.

CHAPTER FOUR

y midmorning the next day, the storm had passed and the sky was a vibrant blue. Snowplows had been busy throughout town, clearing the roads, and Debbie was enjoying a short break between the morning rush and the lunch crowd. No one was in the café except her and Janet, who was running the dishwasher in the kitchen.

Debbie hadn't had a chance to discuss the catering job with Janet. They'd had a steady flow of customers, which meant there had been no time for visiting. As soon as they closed the café, Debbie planned to head over to the museum to chat with Kim about hosting the Homes for Humanity dance in the lobby. She would also ask her about the baby.

The bell over the door sounded, and Debbie looked up from wiping the counter. Kim was helping Eileen through the door. Both women were bundled up in coats, boots, hats, gloves, and scarves. The temperature had dropped significantly behind the snowstorm, and it was bitterly cold out.

"Hello, ladies," Debbie called out, pleased to see them. "This is a pleasant surprise. I was planning to stop by and visit you later, Kim."

"I picked up Mom and took her to my house to look through some of her boxes," Kim said. "We found something she thought you might like, so we decided to stop in to give it to you and enjoy an early lunch together before I take her back."

"Wonderful." Debbie motioned to the chalkboard. "As you can see, we have chicken and dumplings as our special today, but if you'd like something else, I can put in an order for you."

"Chicken and dumplings sounds great," Kim said as she helped Eileen with her coat. "What about you, Mom?"

"Chicken and dumplings is my favorite." Eileen smiled at Debbie. "Can I get a nice hot cup of coffee too? I need to warm up these bones."

"I told you it might be too cold to go out today," Kim said to her.

"Oh, hush." Eileen waved her hand. "I've lived through a hundred Ohio winters. One more won't kill me."

"Mom." Kim shook her head. "The way you talk."

Debbie filled two cups of coffee, knowing Kim would want one too. She brought them to the table her friends chose, close to the counter and away from the chilly windows. "I'll let Janet know you're here."

"Thanks," Kim said as she set a bag on the empty chair next to her. "She'll be interested in the things we brought too."

"Perfect. Be right back."

Debbie passed through the swinging door into the kitchen and found Janet taking out a rack of clean dishes. Steam filled the room.

"Kim and Eileen are here for lunch. Do you have the chicken and dumplings ready?"

Janet nodded. "I'll have a couple of plates prepared in a jiffy."

"They brought something for us too," Debbie said.

"Oh?" Janet raised her eyebrows. "Do you think it has anything to do with the abandoned baby?"

"I don't know, but I hope so."

Debbie left the kitchen and reentered the dining room. "Janet will have your meals out to you soon. Then we can see what you've brought to show us."

"It's not much," Eileen said, "but it helped jog my memory about the baby."

Debbie filled a cup of coffee for herself and brought it to the table. "While we're waiting for Janet," she said, "I'd like to chat with you about an event I'm helping to plan for Homes for Humanity."

Kim set her cup down. "Really? I'd love to hear about it."

Debbie told Kim and Eileen about the dance and how she'd been recruited to help with the event.

"We're wondering if we could use the lobby of the depot," Debbie finished.

"I think it's a wonderful idea!" Kim's face lit up. "I could even keep the museum open that evening, just in case people want to meander through it. You could advertise that the price of the ticket includes admission to the museum."

"That would be great." Debbie grinned. "Thank you."

"A dance brings back so many memories," Eileen said. "I spent hours listening to big-band music in this depot during the war years. We had a dance every Friday night, no matter the weather or season. The locals loved them, and the service members who came in on the troop trains enjoyed a few minutes of fun while they waited for the trains to refuel."

"I'd be happy to help," Kim offered. "Just let me know what I can do."

"I will." Debbie glanced up when Janet entered the dining room with two steaming plates of chicken and dumplings. She wore her apron over a T-shirt that had a picture of a rolling pin and said THIS IS HOW I ROLL.

"That smells delicious," Eileen said. "Why don't you join us too?"

"Let me grab a cup of coffee." Janet did just that and then returned to the table and sat down.

Kim handed Eileen the canvas bag near her feet, and Eileen slowly pulled out a yellowed notebook. "I found this when I went through my old things today. It was one of my school notebooks, but in the back, I have the list of names that I thought could possibly be Baby Sarah's mother. Some of the ink is faded, but most of it is legible." She handed it to Debbie.

"Wow," Debbie said. "Thank you."

"Mom told me the story of the abandoned baby," Kim said. "I hadn't heard about it before, but I'll do some digging and let you know what I find."

"I appreciate that." Debbie opened the notebook and saw math equations in the front. She flipped to the back, where there was a list of four names with a few notes next to each.

Abigail Cobb, Rebekah Lehman, Polly Pinehurst, Betty Harper.

"Those were the four women I suspected," Eileen said. "The first one, Abigail Cobb, was a local teenager who began volunteering at the canteen when the war started. When she didn't show up for her shift one day, I asked around and learned that she had gone to Wisconsin to visit family. She was gone for about six months, and the first time I saw her after that was when she came into the depot moments before Harry found Baby Sarah."

"How old was she?" Debbie asked.

"Probably nineteen at the time Sarah arrived. The second person I suspected," Eileen continued, "was an Amish girl named Rebekah Lehman. She came in on the passenger train that arrived right before the baby was found. When I saw her soon after, she was in the kitchen, already working. She was quiet and skittish and looked as frightened as a cornered rabbit when we questioned her."

Debbie listened carefully to Eileen, making mental notes about these women. One of them might be Aunt Sherry's biological mother—*if* Aunt Sherry was Baby Sarah.

"The third person," Eileen said, "was a farm girl named Polly Pinehurst. She came to Dennison with her father from time to time to drop off produce and whatnot. The last few times I saw her, I noticed that she'd gained weight and taken to wearing bib overalls. I didn't think much about it until she showed up at the depot the very same day as the baby. She and her father had suffered hardships since the war started, and it seemed to change Polly. She wasn't as cheerful or outgoing as she used to be. She came looking for a place to stay too."

"And who was the fourth person?" Kim asked.

Eileen motioned to the notebook. "The next day, I went over the passenger manifesto for the train that had arrived right before Harry found the baby. Only two single women were on it. One was Rebekah Lehman, the Amish girl, and the other was a young woman named Betty Harper. Rebekah stayed in Dennison, but Betty didn't. You can see in my notes that I was able to trace her back to Newark, Ohio, where she'd gotten on the train. I learned that she worked as a maid there. I don't know where she was going. I went to Newark to visit her, but when I got there, I learned she'd been fired from her job that very day and there was no forwarding address."

"You never located her?" Debbie asked.

Eileen shook her head. "Never."

"Hmm." Debbie studied the list of names. "At least this is a start. You believe that one of these young women was the mother?"

"At the time, I apparently did." Eileen shrugged. "I can't recall the details anymore, but I remember being very certain that one of them was Sarah's mother. I could never prove it though."

"Well," Janet said with a smile, "maybe now we can. Who knows what information we'll dig up that wasn't available in 1944?"

"That's what I'm hoping," Eileen said as she looked down at her plate. "Now, I'll dig into this delicious plate of food and tell you all about Abigail, Rebekah, and Polly. They're the ones we questioned first."

Debbie cradled her coffee cup in her hands and settled in to listen to Eileen's story.

February 14, 1944

Mrs. Jefferson had finished feeding the baby and had changed her, using one of the spare diapers she'd brought with her to the depot.

Eileen looked down at the sleeping infant in her arms as she waited for the police officer and the doctor to arrive. The storm continued to rage outside, which probably made it harder for the men to get to the depot. Mrs. Jefferson had gone back to the kitchen, where the volunteers worked at a frenzied pace in preparation for the troop train that should arrive at any minute.

Dr. Powers was the first to walk through the depot doors. The snow blew in with him, leaving a swirl on the wooden floorboards.

He shook his coat and removed his hat. "It isn't fit for man or beast out there today."

Eileen stepped out from behind the ticket counter with the baby in her arms, eager for the doctor to have a look at her. "Thank you for coming."

"Of course, of course. Now. Is this the baby you called about?"

"She's been fed, and her diaper's been changed," Eileen said as she handed the baby over to him. "But we're lucky she's alive."

"My, my." He shook his head. "She's a tiny thing. Where can I examine her?"

A train whistle blew in the distance, signaling to Eileen that the troop train would arrive in less than a minute. "You can use my office, behind the ticket counter."

She hurried him to her office as the canteen volunteers started to pour out of the café. Eileen didn't want the ladies to know about the baby yet. She wanted their full attention to be on the troops they were there to serve.

Eileen left the doctor and closed the office door. She scanned the room to see if Officer Forest had arrived. The lobby would soon be packed, since the service members would come into the depot to look for some warmth. No one would want to stand outside on the platform today.

She didn't see the police officer, so she started to help the ladies bring out the coffeepots and trays of sandwiches and cookies.

While she worked, she looked for the young women Mrs. Jefferson had mentioned. She saw Polly Pinehurst, jaw set, gaze focused on her task. She *also saw Abigail Cobb as she came through the café doors with a tray of sandwiches. But it was the other young woman, Rebekah, who drew Eileen's attention. It was clear she was Amish by her clothing. She wore a white kapp over her dark hair, with strings hanging down to her chest. Her gray dress was plain, as were her black shoes.*

Eileen walked over to Rebekah, ready to question her about her arrival on the last train.

She touched the girl's arm. "Rebekah?"

Rebekah jumped and turned quickly. "Yes, ma'am?"

"I'm Eileen Turner," Eileen said, her voice as gentle as she could make it. "I'm the stationmaster."

"I can tell by your clothes," Rebekah said in a quiet voice.

Eileen looked down at her black skirt and matching blazer. The brass buttons gleamed. She also wore a white collared shirt and a black tie, as well as a black cap. Standard-issue uniform for the stationmaster.

"I heard you arrived on the last train," Eileen said. "There was no need for you to go to work immediately. You can take some time to settle in at the boardinghouse and rest from your travels."

"I came to help," Rebekah said as she resumed pouring coffee. "I don't mind."

A volunteer brought out another large pot of coffee, which Eileen took to help fill the cups. "What brings you to Dennison, Rebekah?"

Rebekah glanced at Eileen and then looked back at the coffee. "Work."

It was easy to sense that Rebekah didn't want to talk, but Eileen had a responsibility to fulfill. Not only as the stationmaster but as a concerned citizen who needed to find the baby's mother. "Do your folks know where you've gone?"

The train chugged into the station, and the activity in the lobby increased.

Rebekah glanced up at the platform doors. She looked petrified—whether from Eileen's questions or from the arrival of the service members, Eileen couldn't tell.

"Are you running away from something, Rebekah?" Eileen asked, setting her hand on Rebekah's arm. "I'm here to help."

Rebekah looked up at Eileen, her eyes wide. "I just want to keep to myself, ma'am."

As the troops started to descend the steps of the train, Rebekah turned and fled into the café.

What was she afraid of?

Eileen worked for the next ten minutes as the lobby filled with hundreds of soldiers. She didn't even notice *when Officer Forest arrived. Suddenly, he was there, at her side, handing out cups of coffee.*

"Thank you for helping," Eileen said.

"Where is the baby?" he asked.

"In my office with Dr. Powers. He's probably staying in there until the lobby clears out."

"Smart man." Officer Forest continued to help hand out coffee until every last service member had been served.

When it was clear that the volunteers had everything under control, Eileen showed Officer Forest into her office where Dr. Powers sat in Eileen's desk chair, staring down at the sleeping baby.

He looked up at their arrival. "She's a little small," he said, "but she appears to be healthy. I don't see anything that concerns me."

"That's a relief," Eileen said as she took the baby from him. "Do you know of anyone in Dennison who could be the child's mother?"

Dr. Powers shook his head. "I don't know of any expectant single mothers, if that's what you mean. I can't imagine a married woman would abandon her baby like this, but I've been surprised by more shocking things in my life."

"I appreciate your help, Dr. Powers," Officer Forest said. "Can you guess the baby's age?"

"*Two or three days at most, judging from the umbilical cord.*"

Officer Forest pulled a small notebook from his breast pocket and made a couple of notes. "*Thank you,*" he said. "*If we have any further questions, I'll be sure to contact you.*"

"*You're welcome.*" Dr. Powers gathered up his bag and said, "*I'll show myself out. Maybe grab a cup of coffee on my way.*"

"*And a sandwich, if you'd like,*" Eileen said. "*I interrupted your supper, and there should be plenty.*"

Dr. Powers nodded and stepped out of Eileen's office.

Officer Forest held his pencil poised over his notebook. "*Tell me everything you know about this baby,*" he said. "*I'll want to speak to Harry as well, and anyone else you think would be helpful.*"

Eileen told Officer Forest everything she could remember and even told him about the young women who had come into the depot that day. When she was done, he looked over his notes.

"*Do you have a passenger list for the train?*" he asked.

"*I have a list of the passengers whose journeys originated here. There were three of them—all men. I can get a passenger manifesto from the other stations along the line, but it will take some time.*"

"That's good. Please let me know when you have it." He glanced toward the door. "I'd like to talk to Harry and the others. Can you ask them to come in here? One or two at a time."

"Of course."

Eileen left the baby in Officer Forest's care and found Harry. She took him to her office, and he told Officer Forest everything he'd already told Eileen. When he was done, Eileen left her office again to look for the young women she suspected. The first one she found was Abigail.

"Can you come to my office, please?" Eileen asked her.

Abigail looked troubled by Eileen's request, but she followed her into the office.

"This is Miss Abigail Cobb," Eileen said.

Abigail froze at the door when she saw Officer Forest and the baby. The color drained from her face, and she leaned against the doorframe as if she had just lost the ability to hold herself up.

"Come in, Miss Cobb," Officer Forest said. He motioned toward Eileen's chair. "I think you need to sit down."

When it looked like Abigail wouldn't be able to walk across the room on her own, Eileen put her arm around her and helped her to the chair.

A sickening feeling churned in Eileen's stomach, and she suspected that they had found the baby's mother.

When Abigail was seated, Officer Forest moved the blanket aside and showed the baby to her. "Is this your child, Miss Cobb?"

Abigail swallowed hard, but she shook her head. "No, sir."

Officer Forest pressed his lips together. "This baby was found freezing on the platform just minutes after you arrived today. Miss Turner tells me you've been away for some time. Visiting family in Wisconsin, was it?"

"Yes, sir." Abigail nodded.

"Did you leave this baby on the platform, Abigail?" Eileen asked gently. Once again, she felt sick, thinking about how desperate the baby's mother must be at this moment.

Abigail turned to Eileen, her eyes distressed, and shook her head again. "No, ma'am. I didn't." Tears slipped down her cheeks. "I could never leave a baby out in the cold. Never."

Though Abigail looked troubled, she also sounded sincere.

Officer Forest asked her several more questions, none of which helped them ascertain if she had left the baby on the platform.

"We may ask to speak with you again, Miss Cobb," Officer Forest said. "if we feel you are, indeed, the mother of this child."

Abigail stared at the police officer. "Am I free to go?"

Officer Forest nodded.

When she was gone, he said, "She's hiding something. I just don't know if it's the truth about this baby. Who else do you think it could be?"

"There are two other young women," Eileen said.

"Bring them in here together, please."

Eileen did as he said. She found Rebekah in the kitchen, washing coffee cups, and Polly in the lobby, picking up sandwich wrappers. Both women agreed to come with Eileen, though they appeared apprehensive.

When they entered Eileen's office and saw Officer Forest standing there, both of them turned just as pale as Abigail had. Polly stiffened, and Rebekah dropped her gaze.

"Girls," Eileen said, "this is Officer Charles Forest. I called him today because this baby was found abandoned on the depot platform. She was discovered soon after the train left that you arrived on, Rebekah. And about the same time that you arrived at the depot, Polly."

Rebekah looked up, her face filled with horror.

Polly's face was like stone.

"Do either one of you know anything about this baby?" Officer Forest asked.

"No, sir," Polly said.

Rebekah shook her head.

"Did you notice anything suspicious when you arrived at the depot?"

Again, they both shook their heads.

"How old are you?" he asked Polly.

"Twenty," Polly said.

He turned to Rebekah. "And you?"

"I'm eighteen," she said.

"Do your parents know where you are?"

Polly's eyes showed a hint of fear for the first time. "I'll be twenty-one next week. My pa can't keep me on the farm forever. I had to get away." She paused, as if she'd said too much.

"And you?" Officer Forest asked Rebekah.

She shook her head. "No, sir. They don't know where I've gone, but they won't be looking for me. I am free to leave the community." She clasped her hands together.

"And neither one of you know where this baby came from?" he asked, squinting at them.

Both shook their heads.

"I'll be contacting you if I have more questions. For now, you may leave."

The girls left the office without looking back.

Officer Forest sighed. "That wasn't helpful."

"What will we do about the baby?" Eileen asked.

He shrugged. "Times are hard on everyone right now. I can contact social services in New Philadelphia, but they won't be able to get here until the storm blows over—and maybe not even then."

"I can take the baby home with me," Eileen said suddenly. She hadn't thought about it. The words had just come out. "I would need some supplies, like diapers and formula, but I think I could manage for a few days."

"And what about when you need to work?" he asked.

"I have a neighbor lady I can ask to help. She has two small children of her own, but I'm sure she wouldn't mind lending a hand for a little while."

Officer Forest looked down at the sleeping infant. "I'll leave her in your care and let you know when I hear from social services. You need to call me if you learn anything else about her mother."

"I will."

He handed the baby to Eileen and shook his head. "It's sad she doesn't have a name."

Eileen studied the baby's face and thought for a moment. "She looks like a Sarah."

"Then Sarah it is—for now." He nodded at Eileen. "I'll be in touch."

As Officer Forest left her office, Eileen ran her finger down Sarah's soft cheek, her heart breaking for the baby and her mother.

CHAPTER FIVE

ebbie listened intently as Eileen told them about the day Sarah had arrived at the depot. As the elderly woman shared what had happened, it appeared to spark more memories for her. She hardly even touched her plate, and Debbie felt bad—but Eileen came alive when she shared stories from her past, and she didn't seem to mind that her food was getting cold.

The bell over the door jingled, and three women entered the café. Debbie didn't recognize them. Since it was her job to serve them, she had to interrupt Eileen as she was telling them about taking Sarah home and caring for her for several weeks as they searched for the baby's mother.

"I'm sorry," Debbie said. She stood from the table and removed her empty coffee cup. "I need to wait on these women, but thank you for sharing what you remember, Eileen."

"You're welcome." Eileen smiled and looked down at her lunch. "I should probably dig into my food."

"I can reheat it for you, if you'd like," Janet offered.

Eileen shook her head. "It's fine. I'm sure it's still warm enough to enjoy."

"Let me know if you change your mind." Janet also stood as another group entered the café.

"I'll tell you if I remember anything else," Eileen said to them.

"I think we have enough to keep us going for a little while," Debbie said. "I'll check into the names you shared and see what I can find."

Eileen nodded and then dipped her fork into her meal and took a bite.

As Debbie took orders, she couldn't stop thinking about what Eileen had shared with them. Eileen had narrowed her suspects down to four young women who could be Sarah's mother—but the truth was, anyone could have walked onto the platform that day and left a baby there. Granted, the likelihood of a stranger coming to Dennison to leave a baby was next to nothing—unless she had come off the train. Which was why Betty Harper was an intriguing suspect. But what happened to her? Why was she fired from her job just before Eileen showed up to question her? It was something Debbie planned to discuss with Eileen when she had more time.

The other three women seemed like strong possibilities too. Each one appeared to be guilty of something—but what? Why had Rebekah left her Amish community? Why had Polly become morose and run away from home? And why had she left a week before her twenty-first birthday?

But, judging from Eileen's story, it was Abigail who had seemed most guilty. Emotional at seeing the baby and so overcome that she couldn't walk across the room by herself? Why had she been in Wisconsin so long?

There were so many questions, but Debbie had to wait until they could close the café to do more digging.

The afternoon was surprisingly busy, given the cold weather and the recent storm. Debbie didn't have a moment to rest until the last customer left for the day. Janet went home, leaving Debbie to do the final cleanup. Since Janet came in early, Debbie often closed for the day. She ran the dishwasher, wiped down the tables, chairs, and counter, and swept and mopped the floors. In the morning, Janet would update the chalkboard menu, do the morning baking, and prep for the breakfast and lunch crowd.

After Debbie put the mop and bucket away, she went to the counter and took a seat. She decided to start her search by looking up Rebekah Lehman. Rebekah was the only single woman who had arrived on the train and stayed at the depot the day the baby arrived.

Debbie pulled out her phone and opened a search engine. She typed in *Rebekah Lehman, Dennison, Ohio.*

None of the links that popped up looked promising, so Debbie added the word *Amish* and then the year 1944. Still, nothing showed up that pointed to the right Rebekah.

Feeling discouraged, Debbie typed in the names Polly Pinehurst, Abigail Cobb, and then Betty Harper. Nothing came up that gave her any leads.

It was a good chance that all of them had married. Their maiden names wouldn't produce the results she needed.

Debbie sighed and looked out the window. There had to be someone else who knew what happened that day.

A familiar figure walked by, causing Debbie to smile.

Of course! Eileen had said that Harry was the one who found the baby. He had lived in Dennison his whole life, worked at the depot for many years, and then went on to ride the trains as a conductor. These days, when the weather was pleasant, he was often on the depot platform with his dog, Crosby. He loved to watch the trains go by, and he especially loved to reminisce with Debbie and Janet about those long-ago days.

Debbie quickly grabbed her coat, hat, and gloves, and then locked the café. She was surprised Harry was outside today, since it was so cold, but then again, it took a lot to keep him away from the depot.

She stepped outside and glanced down the length of the platform to look for Harry. The sun shone on the fresh snow, almost blinding in its intensity.

Harry sat on his favorite bench with Crosby at his feet. When Debbie approached, Harry looked up and grinned.

"Hello," he called, waving his gloved hand.

Thankfully, he was bundled up in a warm coat, gloves, a thick hat, and a scarf. He had boots on his feet and wore snowpants. Even Crosby looked warm in a thick doggie sweater.

"What are you doing out here, Harry?" Debbie asked, shivering. "It's freezing."

"Crosby and I were tired of being cooped up in the house. We both needed a walk. Besides, I don't mind the cold. It doesn't seem to bother him either."

Debbie smiled as she took a seat on the bench next to Harry and slipped off one of her gloves to pet Crosby before putting it back on. Crosby was a white bulldog with a black circle around one of his eyes. Debbie had learned that he was a descendant of Bing, a dog who had lived in the trenches during WWI. Bing had seen active duty, been gassed twice, and was given a standard discharge bonus by the army for his service. He was buried in Dennison's sister city, Uhrichsville.

"How's your day been, Debbie?" Harry asked. His eyes sparkled with joy as he waited for her answer. Debbie always enjoyed Harry's company.

"It's been a busy day in the café—and it's been full of a few surprises. That's why I wanted to come out and chat with you. Do you have a couple minutes to answer some questions I have about something that happened here a long time ago?"

Harry chuckled. "All I have is time. Ask away."

"It's about an abandoned baby that was left on this platform—"

"On Valentine's Day, 1944." He shook his head. "I'll never forget that moment." He pointed to a spot on the far end of the platform. "I found the baby right there, in a small wooden crate. It was the tiniest baby I ever saw—and so blue from the cold. I couldn't believe my eyes. She went home with Eileen, but I got to see her one more time before she was adopted."

"Do you know who adopted her?"

Harry shook his head. "The social services lady came over from New Philadelphia and took the baby to her new home. The adoptive family wanted to remain anonymous, so we never did learn where she went. I always wondered if she stayed close or went far away. I don't think I'll ever know."

Debbie didn't think her aunt Sherry would want her spreading information—especially if it wasn't true. They still didn't know if she was Baby Sarah. There was a lot to uncover before they could know where the baby went and who she had become.

"What else do you remember about that day?" she asked.

He recounted the same story Eileen had told her, with a little more animation.

"Do you know anything about the women Eileen suspected could be the mother?"

Harry shook his head. "Eileen didn't discuss anything about her suspicions with me. She was the stationmaster, and I was only a porter. After I was interviewed by the police officer, I didn't hear much more about the situation, except that the baby had been adopted."

"Do you remember a young woman named Rebekah Lehman?"

Harry squinted and pursed his lips, as if he was thinking.

"She was an Amish girl who came to the depot the same day as the baby," Debbie said.

That seemed to jog his memory. "Oh, that's right! I do remember her. She was a quiet thing, but she stood out to me because she continued to wear her Amish clothing until she got married."

"You remember her getting married?"

Harry grinned. "I was the one who introduced her to her husband, John Potter. He was an acquaintance of mine. He couldn't fight in the war because of some medical reason, though I don't recall what it was now. He was a farmer and was one of the best baseball players I ever saw. I used to go and watch him play when I was younger, and I would hang around to talk baseball with him after the game. That's why I knew him when he came to the depot to donate milk to the canteen. He took a liking to Rebekah from the start, and I was the one who introduced them."

Debbie wrapped her arms around herself to stay warm, eager to hear more.

February 18, 1944

The sky was vibrant blue, but the air was as cold as Harry had ever remembered as he shoveled the roadside walkway in front of the depot. Several farmers who were scheduled to make deliveries in the past couple of days had to hold off because of the storm. But now that it had passed, Harry expected them to show up today.

It was Friday, which meant there would be a canteen dance tonight. Miss Eileen had told him to make sure all the snow was out of the way so people could get in and out of the depot as easily as possible. The canteen relied heavily on the income they brought in from the dance, so she didn't want anyone to turn away because of the snow.

Harry usually whistled as he worked, but it was too cold to do anything but shovel today. It wasn't an easy job, and he breathed hard. At least it kept his blood pumping and helped him to stay warm, though his fingers were frozen and his nose and ears felt like icicles.

As soon as he finished, he set the shovel aside and entered the depot to get a hot cup of coffee and warm up.

It was toasty inside, and Harry was able to remove his gloves and scarf. The Amish girl, Rebekah, stood near the coffee table, cleaning up from the last troop train that had come through. Rebekah was about Harry's age, but something about her made her come across as younger. Inexperienced and vulnerable.

"Hello," he said as he approached the table. "Mind if I help myself to some coffee?"

"Ne. Of course not." Rebekah offered him a rare smile. "Let me pour it for you. My daed's fingers never worked properly when he worked outside. Your hands are likely ice cold."

Harry wouldn't say no to her assistance. He waited as she poured his coffee and handed the cup to him.

"Thank you."

He didn't want her to walk away just yet, so he said, "Do you miss your family?"

Rebekah looked down at her hands and sighed. "Ja."

"Do you plan to go back?"

She shook her head. "I cannot—and I do not want to."

"It isn't easy to be away from the people you love," Harry said. "If you need anything, I'd like to help if I can."

Harry felt a kinship with Rebekah. She was a little older than he was, but they were both trying to make their way in the world. He truly wished he could help her. Though he couldn't think of how. He was already helping his parents pay the bills by working as a porter. He didn't have any extra cash, though Rebekah didn't look like she needed it. The Snodgrass family allowed the canteen girls to board with them for free. After the war, she'd need to find a job, but right now, she had a purpose and a safe place to live.

"Thanks for the hot coffee," Harry said after he took a sip.

"Thanks for listening. I have not spoken of my family to anyone else since I left."

Harry was happy that she'd trusted him. "Are you going to the dance tonight?"

"I do not dance."

He grinned. "Now that you're living among us, you should learn."

Her cheeks turned a deep shade of pink, and she dipped her head. "One thing at a time, ja?"

"I suppose." Harry chuckled, and she picked up a tray of cups to take into the café, tossing him a shy smile over her shoulder as she went.

The day went on like almost all the others before it. The trains came and went, passengers and service members swarmed the lobby, and deliveries were made. Whenever he caught Rebekah's eye, she nodded at him and he felt like he had made another friend.

It was close to five o'clock when Harry saw John Potter enter the depot. He was a tall young man with dark brown hair, and Harry always thought of the actor Tyrone Power when he saw him. John had been a college student before the war, hoping to be an engineer. When the war broke out, he tried to volunteer, but he had a medical condition that prevented him from enlisting. Harry never asked him about it, because he could tell John was embarrassed and ashamed that he wasn't fighting. When his father had asked him to come home and work on the family farm outside Dennison to help in the war effort, John had sacrificed his college education and career to do his part.

But it was his baseball talents that most impressed Harry. Whenever John came to town to play in a local game, Harry always made sure to be there to watch.

"Harry!" John called out with a big grin.

"Hello, John." Harry set aside the broom he'd been using to sweep the dance floor. He had set up the stage they used on Friday nights and rolled the piano over for the band that would come in later. The dances usually got started around seven, so they still had a couple of hours to go. "How's that pitching arm? Keeping it in shape for the spring?"

John grinned. *"You better believe it. I've been throwing snowballs at the garage wall every chance I get. My pa's about had it with the noise."*

Harry laughed.

But John's smile fell. "We lost our catcher, Mike. He turned eighteen and enlisted a week ago."

Harry knew this was a sore spot for John, so he didn't ask any questions about the catcher. Instead, he shifted to a safer subject.

"Gonna stay in town for the dance tonight?"

John shrugged. "I was thinking about it. I just finished with deliveries and have about thirty gallons of milk Pa wants me to donate to the canteen, so I thought I'd stop by here last and see who's around."

"You mean, you thought you'd see if Charlotte is here?"

John grinned.

Charlotte was one of the young women who came over from Freeport to volunteer on a rotating schedule in the canteen. John had met her last time he was in town and had spent much of the night dancing with her.

"Have you spoken to her since the last dance?" Harry asked.

John shrugged. "Nah. Just thought I'd see if she was here. We had a good time, but no promises were made." His gaze shifted, and he seemed to lose his focus on Harry.

Harry turned and saw that Rebekah had reentered the lobby. Her cheeks were pink, and her blue eyes looked bluer than ever.

"Who is that?" John asked, his voice quiet.

"That's Rebekah Lehman. She's boarding in town. Arrived earlier this week."

"Boarding in town?" John asked. "Doesn't she have any family nearby?"

"She left her people," Harry said, not wanting to say much more, since Rebekah had seemed to trust him.

John was quiet. "Can you introduce me?" he finally asked.

"Sure." Harry was happy to make the introduction. He liked John and knew that John was familiar with the Amish. Many of them lived and farmed near his family.

John took off his hat as they approached Rebekah. She had her back to them, so Harry said her name softly, so as not to startle her.

"Rebekah?"

She turned—and her gaze landed on John.

He was much taller than she was, and standing there, holding his hat in both hands, he looked almost nervous.

"Guten Tag," John said to her.

Rebekah's eyes widened in surprise. "Guten Tag," she responded with a smile.

Harry wasn't sure what it meant, but he assumed it was hello. "Rebekah," he said, "this is my friend, John Potter."

"It's nice to meet you, Rebekah," John said.

"Do you know Pennsylvania Dutch?" she asked him.

"Ja." John smiled. "Some. My oncle was Amish before he left the church, and we live close to several Amish families."

Rebekah's face filled with something akin to hope, as if she'd found someone who might understand her.

"Are you going to the dance tonight?" John asked.

"I do not dance."

He smiled again. "I'll teach you."

Rebekah dipped her chin and gave a slight nod.

John looked like he'd just been given a new lease on life.

And Harry smiled as he watched the two of them forget he was even there.

CHAPTER SIX

*D*ebbie was shaking, she was so cold, but she didn't want to interrupt Harry as he told her about Rebekah and John.

"John came to the depot every day for a week." Harry chuckled. "He was smitten, though it took her a little convincing. She'd just given up everything she knew and was making a tough transition. But John was persistent and even brought his uncle to meet her. He had been raised Amish and had left the church to marry John's aunt. I think Rebekah found comfort in meeting someone who had made the change and was happy about it."

Debbie tried not to shiver as she continued to listen.

"They were married a month after they met," Harry said. "I didn't even know about it until it was over and Rebekah didn't come back to work that following Monday."

"Did you ever hear from her again?" Debbie asked.

"I saw John all the time because he continued to deliver milk to town. Rebekah came with him from time to time, and she seemed happy. After the war, John thought about returning to school, but his father died, and he took over the family farm. I think Rebekah was happiest there."

"So her married name was Potter?" Debbie's teeth chattered, despite her best efforts.

"That's right—but you should get on inside," Harry said, looking concerned. "Warm yourself up."

"I think I will." Debbie stood. "Thanks for the information."

Harry grinned. "I'll see you next time I'm in the café."

"Sounds good." Debbie rubbed Crosby's head again and then walked into the depot. She knew her car would be chilly, so she stayed inside for a few minutes to warm up and then went out to head home.

She had wanted to speak to Harry about the other young women, but that would have to wait. At least she had Rebekah's married name and the name of her husband. It might be easier to find information about them.

When Debbie finally reached home, she stood by one of the stand-up radiators in her entryway for a long time to get warm. Her parents and Aunt Sherry were coming over for supper that evening, and she had a lot to do to clean the house and prepare the meal, but she needed to get her fingers and toes working properly again first.

As soon as she felt warm enough, she pulled out her cell phone and typed in the name *Rebekah Lehman Potter*. Both Harry and Eileen had said that Rebekah was eighteen when she appeared at the depot, so that would have put her birth year around 1926. Debbie added that to the search engine, and immediately a genealogical link appeared.

Excitement filled Debbie as she clicked the link and was brought to a page that had the information she needed. It gave the wedding date for Rebekah and John as March 18, 1944. They'd had five children, and all their names and birth dates were listed. The oldest was born in early 1946. It also gave Rebekah's death date as December 28, 2006, and John's as January 18, 2007.

Debbie smiled to herself, thinking about John and Rebekah's marriage spanning over sixty years and then John following Rebekah to heaven just a few weeks after she left.

The website listed one of their grandchildren as the contributor—Andrea Stedman, born in 1982. There was no contact information, so Debbie went to a popular social media site and typed in the name *Andrea Stedman*. There were eight listed. Debbie eliminated several who were either older or younger than the one she was looking for, and eventually she found an Andrea Stedman, age forty-one, who lived in Toledo, Ohio.

"It has to be her," Debbie said as she clicked on Andrea's profile and went through her photos. She had no idea what the correct Andrea looked like, but this woman seemed like the typical soccer mom with posts about her children, her dog, and her house.

There was no way to know for sure without contacting her, so Debbie pressed the message button and typed a note.

Hello, my name is Debbie Albright. I live in Dennison, Ohio, and work at the Whistle Stop Café in the Dennison depot. We are looking for information about a woman named Rebekah Lehman Potter who volunteered briefly here at the Salvation Army canteen in the winter of 1944. I found some information about her online on a genealogy website and saw that the family contributor is an Andrea Stedman. If this is the right Andrea Stedman, would you be willing to message me back? I have a couple of questions and would love to learn more about Rebekah. Thank you!

Debbie reread the message and then pressed send. She hoped this was the right Andrea and that she might have information about her grandmother. It was a long shot, and Debbie wasn't sure what information Andrea might have that would be helpful, but she had to at least try.

She put her phone in her pocket and went into the kitchen and assembled the beef stew. While it was cooking, she ran the vacuum, dusted, and cleaned the downstairs bathroom. The smell of beef and onions filled her house with a warm, delicious aroma.

She often invited her parents over for supper, but because her aunt was away from Dennison for most of the year, this was the first time she had included her. She wanted to tell Aunt Sherry what she had learned about the baby—what little she knew—and had asked her if they could include her parents in on the conversation. Perhaps Dad knew something Aunt Sherry didn't. Aunt Sherry had said she was okay with Mom and Dad coming and telling them what they had discovered.

Debbie was a little nervous, wondering what her dad would think. Maybe he could put all their concerns to rest. Maybe he knew why the crate was in the garage.

By six o'clock, everything was ready for her guests. Debbie had lit a couple of candles, and the smell of pumpkin spice mingled with the spices from the stew. She had crusty bread warming in the oven and the table set.

Her parents were the first to arrive. They pulled into the driveway and came in through the kitchen door.

"Hello." Debbie opened the door a little wider for them to get in out of the cold. Dad held a cake pan with a lid.

"Brr," he said as he walked in. "I made apple crisp for dessert."

Mom followed with a can of whipped cream. "And I brought the topping."

Debbie smiled and quickly closed the door behind them.

"We saw Sherry pulling up to the front of the house," Dad said as he set the apple crisp on the counter. "I didn't realize you had invited her."

"That was nice," Mom added as she took off her coat and set it on the hook near the back door.

"She stopped by the other day with something she found in her garage," Debbie told them. "I thought it would be good for you to see it."

"Oh?" Dad raised his eyebrows. "That sounds intriguing."

The front doorbell rang, and Debbie hurried to open the door for her aunt.

"Hello," she said.

Her aunt smiled. "Thanks for inviting me. I saw your parents just got here."

"Hi, Sherry," Dad said as he entered the foyer with Mom right behind him. "This is a nice surprise."

Aunt Sherry smiled at her younger brother and allowed Debbie to help her with her coat and hat. She and Debbie's dad had never been very close, since thirteen years separated them, but they had stayed connected through the years, especially after their parents died.

Aunt Sherry opened her arms to hug each of them, and then she took a deep breath before she said, "There's something Debbie and I want to talk to you about."

"That's what Debbie said." Dad crossed his arms and studied his sister. "Judging by the look on your face, I don't think it's good news."

"We're not sure if it's even true—yet," Debbie said. "How about we get our food and sit down to discuss it?"

Mom and Dad shared a concerned look, but they followed Debbie back to the kitchen. Everyone dished up their stew in silence, and Debbie brought the bread to the dining room table.

When they were all seated, Dad said a prayer and they began their meal.

Steam rose from their bowls, and the smell of warm bread made Debbie's stomach growl. Everyone ate quietly until Dad finally said, "What's going on?"

Debbie glanced at Aunt Sherry, but she didn't appear ready to speak, so Debbie decided to share the news.

"Aunt Sherry had a neighbor boy help her clean out the garage, and he found a wooden crate in the rafters." Debbie rose to retrieve the crate from the front closet.

She came back and set it at the end of the table, close enough for her parents to see it.

"What is this?" Mom asked, looking from Debbie to Aunt Sherry.

"The crate was originally found on Valentine's Day, 1944, at the Dennison depot," Debbie explained. "Inside was a baby, about two or three days old, who was wrapped in that blanket and wearing that cotton sleeper. An empty bottle, a silver baby rattle, and a newspaper were the only other items with the baby."

"Valentine's Day?" Dad frowned. "It must have been freezing cold. Was the baby okay?"

"She was alive, thanks to Harry Franklin, who found the baby right after a train had left the station," Debbie said. "Eileen Palmer was on duty, and she called the police and a doctor."

"The newspaper in the box tells the story." Aunt Sherry finally spoke up.

"The mother of the baby was never located," Debbie continued, "though Eileen tried to find her for weeks. And then the baby was adopted by an anonymous family through social services in New Philadelphia."

Dad and Mom continued to stare at Debbie, their meal forgotten.

"Why was the crate in your garage?" Dad finally asked Aunt Sherry.

She studied Dad for a heartbeat. "Why do you think, Vance?"

A look of realization slipped over his face, and he went from confused to horrified. "Are you suggesting that you were adopted and our parents never told us?"

"We don't know for sure," Debbie said.

"How *can* we know for sure?" Mom asked.

"I've been thinking about getting a DNA test," Aunt Sherry said. "I looked into it online. If I knew the identity of the birth mother, I could ask her or one of her family members for a saliva sample and I could send in my own. We would have the results back in three to five days."

"And without a possible birth mother?" Debbie asked. "What then?"

"Then it could take three to four weeks to have an ancestry test done, and that would only tell me possible relatives. It wouldn't nec-essarily point me to my birth mother."

"Wait." Dad held up his hands, as if to slow down the conversation. "Sherry, we have no reason to believe you're not my biological sister—other than this crate you found in your garage."

"And the fact that my birthday is February 14, 1944, and that I don't look like anyone else in the family."

Dad was quiet for a moment.

Debbie knew he was processing this information. If Sherry was adopted, then that meant their parents had withheld information—and the truth—from them.

"I'm trying to find the birth mother," Debbie said. "I've spoken to Eileen and Harry, and I might have located the granddaughter of one of the women they suspected could be the birth mother. I'm going to be looking for the other three as soon as I can learn more about them."

"To what end?" Dad asked.

"So we can know who the birth mother is and possibly get a DNA test for Aunt Sherry."

"Do you really want to know?" Dad asked Aunt Sherry. "Can't you just go on like before?"

Aunt Sherry tilted her head at her brother. "If you found out you might be adopted, wouldn't you want to know your birth family?"

"No." Dad shook his head. "I wouldn't."

"Well, I would."

"You and Vance could send in samples," Mom suggested to Aunt Sherry. "At least you would know if you're biologically related to each other. If you aren't, then it would be safe to say you were adopted and that you could very well be the baby who was found on the platform."

Aunt Sherry looked at Dad expectantly. "Would you be willing to do that, Vance?"

Dad didn't meet anyone's gaze. "I'd have to think about it."

"This isn't really your decision," Mom said, putting her hand on Dad's arm. "This isn't about you. It's about Sherry and her wishes. If you don't do it, Debbie could always offer her DNA sample."

Dad pushed his bowl away and stood. "I'm going to need a few minutes to think about this. Excuse me." He walked out of the dining room.

Mom looked from Debbie to Aunt Sherry and shook her head. "He's going to need some time to come to terms with this. But I think, when he does, he'll be willing to help."

Aunt Sherry sighed. "I've had a few more days to accept the possibility. I can't really blame him."

Debbie put her hand on her aunt's back.

None of this was easy, but they had each other, and they would get through it.

A couple of hours later, after everyone had gone home, Debbie flipped off her kitchen light and walked through the dining room into the living room. When Dad had returned to the table, they had spoken about the situation with a little less emotion, though her dad told them he needed more time to think about the DNA test. Debbie could have given a sample, like her mom suggested, but Aunt Sherry wanted to respect Dad's feelings and wait for him to be ready.

Debbie hadn't expected him to be so upset, but she understood. If Sherry were her sister, she'd be struggling too.

It was too early to go to bed, so Debbie sat on her couch and opened a book she'd been reading.

But her mind was too busy to focus on the story. She had checked her social media account several times to see if Andrea Stedman had read her message and responded, but there was still no answer. She had hit a dead end with the names of the other women and didn't know where to look for more information. She needed to talk to Harry again to see if he knew anything about them, but the odds weren't in her favor. Thousands of women came through the depot in the 1940s. How was Harry expected to remember these particular ones?

Debbie contemplated this as she read the same paragraph for the fifth time. She was startled when her phone rang. Lifting it off the end table, she was surprised and happy to see Greg's name on the screen.

She pressed the talk icon and said, "Hello?"

"Hi, Debbie. Are you busy?"

"No." She closed the book and set it aside. "What can I do for you?"

"I'm just a couple blocks away. Can I stop by to talk about the dance?"

"Sure. Come on over."

"Great. See you soon."

A few minutes later, a set of headlights flashed against the back wall of Debbie's living room. She met Greg at the front door with a smile and was surprised to see that Jaxon and Julian were with him.

"Thanks for letting us stop by," he said as they came into the house. "Jaxon had a basketball game this evening, and we just got done."

"Did you win?" Debbie asked Jaxon.

He nodded, grinning. "By a lot."

"Good for you. You'll have to let me know when you have your next home game. I'd love to come."

"You can check out the schedule on the school website," Julian offered helpfully.

"I'll have to do that." Debbie motioned for them to come into the living room. "Are you guys thirsty?"

"I'll take some water, please," Jaxon said.

Greg laughed. "He could drink from a fire hydrant after a game and not get enough," he said.

"I'll get all of us some water," Debbie said.

"I can help," Greg offered.

The boys stayed in the living room while Greg followed Debbie into the kitchen.

"How are the plans coming for the dance?" Greg asked.

Debbie opened a cabinet door and pulled out four glasses. "I've reserved the lobby of the depot, and Kim has offered to keep the museum open that night for people to wander through. She said we can advertise that the price of admission is included in the ticket price."

"That's awesome." Greg smiled. "I'll tell Marnie to start advertising immediately. With social media and our email newsletter, we shouldn't have any trouble letting the community know about the change in plans."

"I spoke to Janet. She's happy for us to cater the event. And, despite your protests, we want to donate our time."

"I appreciate that."

Debbie filled the glasses with ice cubes. "What about the band?"

"I contacted the band leader, and he said they're free that night."

"That's great."

"I told him I'd like to hear them play before we hire them, which is one of the reasons I wanted to stop by and talk to you. They'll be performing next Friday evening in Canton, and I was wondering if you were free to go with me to check them out. It's a charity dance at the Onesto, open to the public, so we're welcome to attend."

Canton was about a forty-minute drive from Dennison, and the Historic Onesto was a stunning venue. Debbie thought through her schedule and couldn't think of anything she had planned for Friday.

"I'm free," she said. "I'd enjoy going with you."

Greg's smile was so sweet, it warmed Debbie's heart.

"Great." He nodded. "It's a date—I mean—you know what I mean."

Debbie laughed. "I know what you mean."

Jaxon walked into the kitchen and looked between Debbie and Greg, his gaze full of curiosity and irritation. Whenever Debbie and Greg appeared to be flirting—or getting close—Jaxon made it obvious he didn't like the idea. And Debbie wasn't about to get between a son and his father.

She turned to the sink to fill the glasses. She could almost imagine the look Jaxon gave to his dad behind her back.

When the glasses were full, she handed one to Jaxon and one to Greg and then carried the other two into the living room, where she handed one to Julian.

They stayed to visit for a few minutes, but it was getting late, and everyone had church in the morning. And after the awkward moment in the kitchen, Jaxon remained edgy. Debbie and Greg didn't discuss going to Canton anymore, but they did talk about the fundraiser, and Greg told Debbie about the marketing efforts that Marnie would be making to promote the event.

Jaxon was fidgety, and Greg finally said it was time to head home.

Debbie walked them to the door and said good night. Greg was the last one to leave the house, and right before he closed the door, he offered Debbie a gentle smile, as if apologizing for Jaxon.

She returned the smile and nodded, trying to communicate that she was okay.

When they were gone, Debbie locked the doors, turned off the lights, and headed up to bed with her book.

She didn't feel like she had made much progress with her quest to find Baby Sarah's birth mother, and she had a lot to do for the fundraiser. At the moment, she felt a little overwhelmed by it all.

After putting on her pajamas and brushing her teeth, she climbed into her comfy bed and tried to tune it all out and bury herself in her book.

CHAPTER SEVEN

On Monday afternoon, Debbie was wiping a table in the café when the door opened and her dad walked in.

"Hey, Dad." She straightened up and smiled at him. There was an older couple at a table in the corner. They had already paid and were drinking the last of their coffee, but the rest of the café was quiet.

"Hey, kiddo." He took off his coat and hung it on the coat tree by the door. "Can I get a cup of coffee?"

"Sure." Debbie finished wiping the table and then went to the counter to grab a cup and fill it with the steaming brew. "What brings you in here today?"

Dad took a seat at the counter, not appearing to hear her question. His shoulders were stooped as he pulled the cream and sugar toward himself.

Sunshine poured into the windows behind him, framing him in a swath of light. Debbie knew he was here to talk about Sherry, but she didn't want to push him.

"Hungry?" she asked, trying to draw him out again.

He glanced at the bakery cabinet and shook his head. "I think the coffee will be good for now."

The other couple stood and waved to Debbie, put on their coats, and left the café.

It was now just the two of them. Janet was in the kitchen, cleaning up from the lunch rush.

Dad took a sip of his coffee, apparently in no hurry to tell her why he had come.

Debbie leaned against the back counter and watched him. "Are you going to talk about it?"

"Why does she want to know?" he finally asked. "Why not leave well enough alone?"

"She might be adopted, Dad. And, more than that, she might be the baby abandoned on the depot platform. That must pose a lot of questions for her." Debbie shrugged. "Besides, none of us know what we'd do in that situation, so we can't judge her. It might be easy to say what you would do, but it's not you."

"My parents aren't here to defend themselves. If they *did* adopt Sherry, and they chose not to tell her, we'll end up with more questions than answers. We'll never know why they decided not to tell us. I don't want to be angry at them for keeping the truth to themselves."

"You don't have to be angry. If it's true, then I'm sure they had their reasons. It doesn't change the facts though. If she was adopted, and they chose not to tell her, it might hurt—but reality is reality. Just because you don't know doesn't mean it's not true."

Dad fiddled with the handle of the cup. "Ignorance is bliss, I guess."

Debbie moved closer. "She's going to look for the answers, one way or another. It would be nice if you'd help her. This has the potential to change her life, and she could use some encouragement and support right now."

He let out a loud sigh. "I guess you're right. Whether she was adopted or not, it doesn't change how we feel. She's still my sister, and I still love her."

"And your parents loved her too," Debbie added. "But this is a big *if*. We don't know anything yet."

"I'll stop by her house when I leave here and let her know I'll cooperate."

"That'll make her happy. Thanks, Dad."

He nodded. "Do you think you'll discover the truth about the baby's birth mother?"

"I'm trying my hardest. Janet and I are going to Good Shepherd today to visit with Eileen again. She called and said she remembered some details about the women she suspected back then. I'm hoping she can tell me their married names. That would be helpful as I try to track them down."

"Good. Let me know if I can do anything to help, and say hi to everyone there for me."

"I will. Tell Aunt Sherry I'm doing my best."

Dad took another sip of his coffee. "Go ahead and do what you need to do. I don't want to keep you from your work."

Debbie smiled and went to bus another table while he finished his coffee.

Two hours later, Debbie and Janet were on their way to see Eileen.

"Greg stopped by with the boys last night," Debbie said as they got out of the car in the Good Shepherd parking lot. She had been thinking about Greg's visit most of the day but hadn't mentioned it yet. She wasn't quite sure what to make of it.

"Oh?" Janet lifted an eyebrow. "For anything important?"

It hadn't really been an important reason—and Greg could have just called or texted her about an update—but he'd stopped by. Was he looking for a reason to see her? Debbie didn't want to get her hopes up. She didn't want to be disappointed if he really did stop by just to talk about the fundraiser.

"He wanted to talk about the dance. I told him we'd be happy to cater the event." They walked side by side up the sidewalk, though it was a little narrower because of the snowbanks on either side. "He also found out the band we're thinking about hiring is playing this Friday night in Canton, and he asked me to go with him to check them out."

"Really?" Janet looked more curious now. "Like a date?"

"No. Not a romantic date, anyway. We're only going to listen to the band."

"Just the two of you?"

Debbie shrugged. "I guess."

Janet raised her eyebrows. "And where is this dance in Canton?"

"The Onesto." Try as she might, Debbie couldn't suppress a tingle of excitement.

Janet didn't say anything as she opened the door. All she did was smile.

They entered the building and were greeted by the receptionist at the front desk. "Good morning, ladies," she said. "Eileen told me to let you know that she and Ray are in the sunroom."

"Thank you, Ashley." Debbie loved the sunroom. Her dad had it built about five years ago. It jutted out of the south side of the property, and the walls were floor-to-ceiling windows, almost like an atrium. Even the ceiling was wall-to-wall windows. It allowed the residents to feel like they were outside, even on days like today, when the temperature was low and the snow made it difficult to maneuver.

Debbie and Janet signed in and then followed the hallways to the south side of the building. The sunroom was filled with daylight, and dozens of plants were situated throughout the area. Some on the ground, some on stands, and some hanging from the ceiling. Quite a few residents were gathered there, chatting, playing cards, or sitting with a book or needlework project in hand.

Eileen was watering a plant while Ray sat in his wheelchair, watching.

"Hello," Debbie said as she entered. "That's a beautiful plant."

"I brought it from home." Eileen set the small watering can down. "I was so happy they had a place for it to live when I moved in. It's called a monstera plant."

"It looks tropical," Janet commented, admiring the large-leafed plant.

"It is." Eileen motioned to the small table near her plant. "Thanks for coming out here again. I know you ladies are busy."

Debbie took a seat and smiled at Ray. "We're thankful that you're willing to tell us what you remember about the baby. I hope we're not bothering you."

"Of course not," Eileen assured her. "I love talking about the old days. Makes me feel young again."

"And we all enjoy that," Ray added with a twinkle in his eye.

The room was surprisingly warm, even though the snowy landscape on the other side of the windows looked like a frozen wonderland.

"I brought you some treats from the café." Janet set a bakery box on the table.

"Oh." Ray reached for the box. "I don't mind if I do."

"You'll ruin your supper, Raymond Zink," Eileen scolded.

He grinned at her. "I'm ninety-eight years old. If I want to ruin my supper, I think I have the right to ruin my supper."

Debbie and Janet smiled at each other, and Debbie hoped that if she made it to ninety-eight, she'd be as happy as Ray and Eileen.

"I suppose you're curious about why I called you here," Eileen said after giving Ray a look.

Debbie leaned forward. "We'd love to know if you recall anything else. After work yesterday, I had a chance to talk to Harry about Rebekah Lehman. He remembered she'd married a man named John Potter."

"That's right," Eileen said. "I'd forgotten they were married. So many people came in and out of the depot over the years, it's hard to keep track."

"I'm amazed at what you remember." Janet shook her head in awe.

"I don't know how much this will help," Eileen cautioned, "but I remembered something about Polly Pinehurst's story. I was taking care of Baby Sarah and working full-time at the depot. My neighbor helped during the day, but in the evenings and at night, I was the primary caregiver. It was a special time, but I wasn't prepared for how hard it was. I was sleep-deprived and anxious to find her mother. I'm surprised I remember anything from those days."

"Whatever you remember will be important," Debbie assured her.

"It happened early in the morning, when I first got to the depot, about four or five days after Sarah arrived."

Debbie listened eagerly. If the baby was her aunt Sherry, she wanted to know everything she could about her arrival at the Dennison depot.

February 19, 1944

Eileen leaned against the table in the depot lobby, clutching her cup of coffee like it was an anchor—or maybe a buoy. It was the only thing that kept her standing upright. If it wasn't for the caffeine, she was sure she'd lay her head down on her desk and fall asleep for the rest of the day.

She had never felt more exhausted in her life. Sarah had spent most of the night crying, and Eileen didn't know how to meet the baby's needs. Her neighbor was helpful during the day, but at night, all the responsibility fell on Eileen's shoulders. She had been the one to offer to take on the baby—a fact she constantly reminded herself of.

The lobby was blessedly quiet this morning. They'd woken up to another snowstorm. This one wasn't as strong as the last, and it wasn't as cold, but the snow fell outside in a steady, silent curtain of white.

Eileen took another sip of her coffee as Polly came into the lobby with a tray of sandwiches.

She paused when she saw Eileen standing there.

"Morning," Eileen said. She tried not to look accusingly at any of the young women they had questioned the day Sarah arrived at the depot, though she couldn't help but study them when their paths crossed. She had spoken to Officer Forest a few times, but they had no new leads, and the New Philadelphia social worker who had contacted Eileen hadn't come for the baby yet. She said if Eileen was willing to take care of Sarah for now, she'd try to find a more permanent situation as soon as possible.

"Morning," Polly responded as she set the tray on the table. They were preparing for the next troop train, due in about twenty minutes.

Polly glanced toward the doors of the depot. Eileen had noticed her doing this each time she came into the lobby. The look of apprehension on her face was heart-tugging, as if Polly expected something—or someone—to come through that door at any second and drag her away.

"How are you getting along, Polly?" Eileen asked, trying to forget how tired she felt or how much she *wanted a nap. And it was only eight o'clock in the morning.*

"I'm doing fine," Polly said.

"Are you comfortable at the Snodgrass house?"

Polly nodded, pushed the tray to the back of the table, and then started to walk toward the café.

"If you need anything," Eileen said, "you can ask me."

"Yes, ma'am." She pushed through the door, leaving Eileen alone in the lobby again.

Eileen sighed.

The main door opened, and she turned to see who had come.

A man entered. He was tall and broad, with a heavy beard and worn clothing. Snow covered his hat and shoulders and was caked on his rubber boots.

Eileen instantly recognized him, and her heart started to pound.

"Where's Polly?" he growled. He stared at Eileen, and hatred and anger radiated off him like steam from a locomotive engine.

Eileen wasn't sure how to answer. Polly was his daughter, yet it was clear she had left home, and Eileen assumed she didn't want him to know she was there. If she was in danger, Eileen needed to protect her.

"What can I do for you, Mr. Pinehurst?" Eileen asked, hoping Polly didn't come out of the café while he was standing there.

"I want my daughter. I've looked all over the county for her. She has to be somewhere. She shouldn't be alone—not now."

"Why would you think she's here?"

Mr. Pinehurst walked across the lobby to tower over Eileen. He left clumps of muddy snow in his wake, but he didn't seem to care. "I've looked everywhere I can think of. If she isn't here, then she probably came through here to buy a train ticket. I know you know where she's at."

Eileen realized she could use this situation to get more information about Polly if Mr. Pinehurst was willing to share it.

"Did she run away?" she asked.

"Five days ago. She was desperate and unwell. She should be at home, and if I find her, I'll make sure she never leaves again. She doesn't know what she's doing, especially in her condition."

Her condition? What did that mean? Was Mr. Pinehurst all but admitting that Polly had been pregnant?

She knew a little about the Pinehursts' story, though they kept to themselves. A few years ago, the *family came into town for church on a regular basis and had appeared happy and well-cared for. But then the war started, and Polly's older brother left to fight. Then Mrs. Pinehurst died, and shortly after word came that Polly's brother had died in battle. After that it was just Polly and her father on the farm. They stopped coming to church, and Eileen rarely saw Polly in town at all. The few times she had seen her, Polly seemed very unhappy.*

"I'm sorry you've been having trouble," Eileen said. "Do you think Polly is in danger? Was she sick?"

"No. Nothing like that." He frowned and looked beyond Eileen toward the café.

"Did you ask for help from the police?" Eileen asked, wondering if Officer Forest had told him that he'd seen Polly at the depot.

"I don't need their help. I can find her on my own. Now, is she here or not?"

Eileen made a choice, one she prayed she wouldn't regret. "I can't help you, Mr. Pinehurst. If I see Polly, I'll tell her I spoke to you. If she wants to go home, I'm sure she will."

Mr. Pinehurst stared at Eileen, his face filled with rage. Yet, behind his eyes, Eileen saw the grief he tried to hide with his anger. "If I find out you're helping her, I won't take too kindly to your meddling, Miss Turner."

Eileen had put up with a lot as a young, female stationmaster. She wasn't afraid of Mr. Pinehurst. She stared at him, unwilling to bend to his bullying.

With another growl, Mr. Pinehurst left the depot and slammed the door closed.

Eileen sighed and turned toward the café to talk to Polly.

She found her washing cups at the sink and tapped her on the shoulder. "Can I have a word with you?"

Polly's eyes were wide as she nodded.

Eileen led Polly out of the café, hoping Mr. Pinehurst wouldn't burst into the lobby again.

By the time they got to Eileen's office, Polly's back was stiff and she looked leery, though she didn't seem frightened. Whether she was or not, Eileen didn't know. Polly often hid her true feelings behind a mask of indifference.

"Have a seat, Polly," Eileen said.

"Is this about that baby?" Polly asked. "It wasn't me. That's not my baby."

"Please sit." Eileen took her own seat and studied Polly as she sat opposite her. "Your father was just here."

The expression that came over Polly's face was nothing short of panic. She gripped the armrests of her chair and looked toward the door as if he'd appear at any moment.

"I told him I couldn't help him find you," Eileen assured her. "I didn't tell him you're here, but he said he's searched everywhere else, and I think he's narrowed down your location."

"I'm not going back home." Polly shook her head. "He can't make me after I turn twenty-one tomorrow."

"Why didn't you wait until your birthday to leave?"

Polly stared at her lap. She wore the same overalls she'd been wearing when she arrived several days ago, and Eileen wondered if she had anything else with her. She wasn't getting paid to volunteer, and though she didn't have to pay for her room and board at the Snodgrass house while she worked at the canteen, she would need money for other necessities.

"I couldn't stay there another day," Polly said quietly.

"Things must be hard since you lost your brother and mother."

"You have no idea." She pressed her lips together. "Dad's become someone different. I don't even know him anymore."

She paused, and tears gathered in her eyes.

"Has he hurt you, Polly?"

She took a deep breath. "No, but he won't let me out of his sight. He's afraid I'm going to die too." She shook her head. "I couldn't stay there another minute.

He doesn't let me have friends, or date, or even go into town to shop by myself. The only place I could go was church—but he put a stop to that too. I'll shrivel up and die if I have to stay in that house for the rest of my life."

Eileen finally understood. "I'm sorry it's been so hard on you, Polly."

"When he found out I was secretly dating a boy from church, he locked me in my room. I just can't live like that anymore."

"Does your boyfriend know you're here?"

Polly shook her head. "I haven't told anyone I'm here. I want to wait until my birthday, so Dad can't force me to go back with him. I just have to hide out for one more day. I'm going to let my boyfriend know tonight."

"The way he came in here tells me he won't care if it's your birthday tomorrow. He'll try to get you home, no matter how old you are."

"Then I'll call the police. After I'm twenty-one, he won't have any legal rights to me." Her face was hard. "I won't go back there."

Eileen studied the girl. She'd already asked her if the baby was hers, and Polly had denied it.

Polly sniffed. "Can I go now?"

Eileen nodded. She wasn't sure if Polly was being completely truthful about the baby, but she knew the girl was desperate. And desperate people did desperate things.

She wouldn't dismiss the possibility of Polly's involvement with Sarah's birth. Not yet.

CHAPTER EIGHT

W hat happened after that?" Debbie asked as Eileen finished her story. "Did her father take her home? Was she pregnant?"

Eileen shook her head. "She did not return home. I remember that much. After she turned twenty-one, her father knew he couldn't force her home without facing criminal charges." A deep sigh escaped Eileen's lips. "I'm afraid things didn't go well for him though. He died a miserable recluse on his farm a couple of years later. I heard that Polly inherited the property, but she sold it without returning there. At least, that's what people said. I didn't see her after she left the depot."

"When did she leave?" Janet asked. "Right after her birthday?"

Eileen nodded. "She didn't come back to the depot after that day. When I asked about her, Mrs. Snodgrass said that a young man arrived at her house on the morning of Polly's birthday and he took her away."

"Do you know his name?" Debbie asked. "Did she marry him? Was he her boyfriend?"

"I don't know." Eileen shook her head again. "I didn't hear about her after that—other than when her father died and someone said she sold the farm."

"I wonder if her name is on record at the county recorder's office in New Philadelphia," Ray said. "If she sold the property, her name must be on the deed. And it might be her married name, since it was a few years later."

Debbie smiled at him. "You're right! That's brilliant, Ray. Thank you."

"I'd be happy to run over there today and check," Janet offered. "We just need the address of the property. Do you remember where it was?" she asked Eileen.

"I do," Ray said. "I remember Mr. Pinehurst coming to the depot before I left for the war. He was an amiable fellow, before his wife died. We talked about his farm all the time. I even made deliveries there for him. He paid me well." Ray told them where the farm was located, and Debbie was able to pull it up on her maps app to find the exact address.

"This is perfect," she said. "Thank you so much."

"Hopefully, Polly is easier to find with her married name," Eileen said.

"That's what I'm counting on," Debbie said. "Do you recall anything else about Abigail Cobb or Betty Harper that might be helpful?"

Eileen closed her eyes, as if she was deep in thought. When she opened them, she shook her head. "I don't know much about Abigail Cobb. She was such a quiet thing. I could never get her to talk to me. After she came back from Wisconsin, she was even more reserved. Maybe Harry knows something about her. He seemed to have a better comradery with the volunteers than I did. I'd ask him."

"And Betty?" Janet asked.

"I searched for her in Newark, but like I said, she was already fired from her job. I wish I could remember the details, but I can't recall her employer's name or anything else about her. If I hadn't seen her name in that notebook I gave you, I wouldn't have even remembered that much. But I'll keep looking through my things and see if I can find something that jogs my memory."

"We appreciate that," Debbie said. "Every little bit helps."

"I know you do." Eileen smiled. "I'm happy to help when I can."

Debbie and Janet said their goodbyes, promising to keep Eileen and Ray informed if they learned anything new.

When they got to the parking lot, Janet said, "Is it my imagination, or has the temperature dropped again?"

Debbie shivered. "I think it's getting colder."

They got into Debbie's car, and she turned on the motor. As soon as the heater kicked in, she cranked the fan to get as much heat as she could.

Her phone dinged before she started to pull out of the parking lot, so she took it out of her purse and glanced at the screen.

"I just got a message from Rebekah Lehman Potter's granddaughter!" Excitement warmed Debbie better than the heater ever could.

"What does she say?" Janet asked.

Debbie opened the message and read it out loud.

"'Thank you for reaching out to me. I never expected to hear from someone connected to Gram's past. I'm not on social media often, so I just got the message now. Sorry for the late reply. I'm so excited to connect with you! Gram died when I was twenty-four, and so I had many good years with her. She often talked about

Dennison, because she said it was there that her second life started. She met Granddad, and it was love at first sight. She told me it was at the depot that she left the old behind and found her future. Isn't that sweet? We all loved Gram and Granddad so much. Losing them so close together was bittersweet.

"'I don't know if I have any information you want, and I'm not sure what you're looking for, but I would love to stop by the depot and talk with you. I've been meaning to get there to see it for myself, and this was a good reminder. Gram had a diary that she brought with her from the farm where she grew up, and she kept it going until a few months after she married Granddad. After that, she said she was too busy raising babies and caring for the farm to keep it up. I'll be sure to bring it with me. There are a lot of insights into her life when she was with the Amish community and the reason she left.

"'I have a day off work tomorrow. Can I come, perhaps midafternoon? Would you be available to meet? Andrea.'"

"She wants to come tomorrow?" Janet asked.

"That's what it sounds like." Debbie pressed the reply button. "Tomorrow is good for me. I could show her around the depot and the museum after we close. Are you available?"

"I should be." Janet smiled. "I'd like to meet her."

"I'll let her know." Debbie quickly typed a reply, telling Andrea they'd love to see her and get a peek at the diary. "Maybe the diary will tell us what brought Abigail to Dennison and whether or not she brought the baby with her."

"I can't wait to see it."

"Neither can I." Debbie finished her message and then put her phone back into her purse.

"You don't mind running to New Philadelphia this afternoon to the recorder's office?" Debbie asked as she pulled out of the parking lot.

"Not at all."

"I would come with you, but I have a Homes for Humanity meeting. We'll be discussing the fundraiser dance."

"It's okay." Janet shrugged. "I don't mind going alone."

"Thanks."

Debbie had to force herself to shift her thoughts toward the upcoming meeting. She had a lot of things she wanted to discuss with the board, and she wasn't sure if she'd get approval. The few emails she'd sent to Marnie hadn't seemed well received, and Debbie was convinced that no matter what she suggested, Marnie would be against it. It was frustrating, to say the least, but Debbie was willing to put up with it if it meant helping the organization.

It didn't hurt that she was excited to see Greg again. Any reason to be in his company was a good reason.

Debbie didn't have much time after she dropped Janet off at the depot before she had to get to the meeting. When she got there, she saw Greg's truck parked out front, and even though she'd known he would be there, her stomach filled with butterflies.

It was a strange reaction, and one Debbie hadn't anticipated. She'd been attracted to Greg from the moment she met him, but she had forced herself not to let her heart get too involved. Not only was Greg a single dad with teenage boys, but she was just starting over herself. It was a huge undertaking to buy a house and open a new business in her hometown. She wanted to focus her time and attention on the investments she'd made in the café.

The only trouble was, she didn't know how long she could use that as an excuse. The real truth of the matter was simple. Even though she'd recently decided to look to the future instead of dwelling in the past, she was scared—scared to give her heart to someone again. Losing Reed was the most devastating thing that had ever happened to her, and she wasn't sure she could go through it again. She liked Greg, but it was easier to keep herself at a distance and not take the risk.

She reminded herself of this as she parked her car and walked into the building.

Greg sat at the conference table with Marnie. She leaned toward him, pointing to something on a piece of paper. Her laughter grated on Debbie's nerves just a little too much, and she had to force herself to smile at the pair when they looked her way.

"Hey, Debbie," Greg said, rising from his chair to greet her.

Marnie stayed seated and pulled the papers together, ignoring Debbie.

"Hi," Debbie said.

"Here, let me take your coat." Greg approached and took it from her. It wasn't necessary, but it was a kind gesture and made Debbie feel appreciated and welcomed.

"Thank you." She smiled at him and was rewarded with his dimpled smile in return.

As he hung her coat on the coatrack, Debbie approached the table. "Hello, Marnie."

"Oh, hi." Marnie glanced up, as if she was surprised to see Debbie.

There were blueprints on the table, and Debbie made herself busy studying them.

"This is the house we're planning to build in the spring for the Torrez family," Greg said. He returned to the table and moved the blueprints so Debbie had a better view of them. He pointed to the kitchen. "Marnie and I were just discussing the changes that Gabe and Sonia are requesting for the kitchen area. They have a large extended family and are hoping for a different layout to accommodate their gatherings."

"I don't think we can do it," Marnie said. "The lumber has already been ordered—"

"But I think we can," Greg interrupted. Debbie detected a bit of impatience in his voice. "As I just said, it won't be more work, since we haven't even started the project. We'll just need to adjust a few of these walls. It shouldn't be a problem."

Marnie shrugged. "I'm only the project manager—not the contractor. I'll have to leave it in your hands, I guess."

Debbie couldn't stop herself from saying, "They're very capable hands."

Greg's smile was appreciative—if not a little embarrassed—but Marnie's stare was cool.

The front door opened, and a couple of the other board members came in. The meeting wasn't supposed to start for a few minutes, so everyone visited while they waited.

"Can I get you some coffee?" Greg asked Debbie.

"Sure." She wasn't interested in staying at the table alone with Marnie, so she said, "I'll join you."

They walked to the other side of the room where the coffee maker sat on a cart.

"Cream and sugar, right?" Greg asked as he picked up the carafe.

"Yes, please," she replied, happy he knew that. After he doctored her coffee, he handed it to her, and their fingers brushed. She glanced up at him—and found his gaze on her.

It lasted no more than a second, but it warmed her to the soles of her feet.

"I'm excited about the dance on Friday," Debbie said, looking for something to say to fill the silence between them.

"So am I. It's nice that the boys are old enough to stay home alone now. I don't have to worry about finding a babysitter anymore." He poured himself a cup of coffee and added cream and sugar. "I'm starting to get a taste of empty nesting, though, and I'm not sure how I feel about it. The boys are both hanging out with friends this afternoon and won't be home until after supper. It's strange not to have them home when I get there."

Debbie's pulse picked up speed at the thought that popped up, and before she lost her nerve, she asked, "Would you like to go out for pizza after the meeting? I don't have plans for supper."

He glanced at her, and Debbie wondered what was going through his mind. This was more like a date than the dance. Would he think she was too forward?

"We can use the time to talk about the fundraiser," she added quickly, her cheeks feeling warm.

"Sure." He nodded. "I'd like that."

"Great." Debbie's whole body felt warmer than normal, as if someone had cranked up the heat. Was it going to be awkward to have supper alone with Greg? What if they didn't have anything to talk about? What if they had everything to talk about and it became harder to protect her heart from her feelings for him?

"We should get the meeting started," Marnie called, interrupting the conversations that were filling the room with chatter.

Greg motioned for Debbie to precede him back to the table.

Debbie held her cup in both hands, blowing across the surface to give herself something to do to calm her nerves. How could she focus on the meeting, knowing that she and Greg were going out for pizza afterward? Alone?

"I'd like to call the meeting to order," Marnie said a couple of minutes later after everyone was seated. Since it was a subcommittee meeting to plan the fundraiser, they didn't need to go through the minutes or the treasurer's report.

"Let's get right down to business," she said. Her gaze roamed the table, but she avoided looking at Debbie. "Greg has told me that we have a venue for the dance—the depot—and that he has a tentative hold on a band that he will be checking out this Friday in Canton. I've also been told that we have a caterer and that the menu has been decided per our conversation at the last meeting."

The entire time she spoke, she directed her words toward Greg and not Debbie, even though Debbie had been the one to offer the depot for the venue and her and Janet's services for the catering. Marnie was acting like Debbie had nothing to do with either.

"I've started to market the changes to the event," Marnie continued.

"And we've begun to sell tickets," Lexi added. "People seem really excited about it."

There were murmurs of approval around the table.

"I've been in contact with a dancing club from Akron," said another board member. "They're a swing dancing club, and they're excited to come. They've told their club members about it, and we should be getting more ticket sales from them. They've even agreed to do some dancing demonstrations for us that evening if we'd like."

"That's a wonderful idea," Debbie said with a smile. "I've heard of them. They dance in period clothing, don't they? From the 1940s?"

The man nodded. "I saw them at a different event I attended last wee—"

"That's all well and good," Marnie interrupted. "But we need to stay on task so we can get this meeting over as soon as possible."

Debbie smiled at the man who had shared the information to encourage him that it was a good idea.

"We'll need a decorating committee," Marnie said. "Is anyone familiar with 1940s decorations?"

"How about we decorate with an American theme?" Debbie suggested. "Since we're celebrating the 1940s and that was a time of great patriotism, because of the war. We could decorate kind of like a USO event with red, white, and blue bunting, stars, and streamers."

"This is a Valentine's Day event," Marnie said, as if Debbie were a small child. "Not a Fourth of July event."

"That's true," Greg said, "but we are trying to recreate a 1940s dance—and it would have been natural for them to decorate in red, white, and blue. I think it's a great idea. We want people to feel like they've gone back in time, don't we? What better way than to throw a USO-themed dance?"

Debbie appreciated that he was going to bat for her again.

"I like it," said the man who had suggested the dancing demonstrations. "It sounds just about perfect."

The others voiced their agreement, and it appeared that Marnie was outvoted again.

She pressed her lips together and then said, "Okay. It seems I'm not going to get anywhere with this. Since it's your idea, Debbie, are you willing to head up the decorating committee?"

"Sure." Debbie wouldn't back down now. "I'd be happy to."

"I'll let you know our budget for decorations," Marnie told her. "But we need to move on to other topics."

As Marnie led the rest of the meeting, Debbie let her mind wander over the ideas she had for decorating the lobby of the depot.

Soon, the meeting came to an end, and Greg went for their coats. He brought Debbie's to her, and she thanked him.

"Greg," Marnie said, "I was hoping you could stay for a few minutes to finish our discussion about the Torrez kitchen."

"I'm sorry, Marnie. Debbie and I made plans to go out for supper. We can finish the conversation tomorrow when we meet with Gabe and Sonia."

Marnie lifted her chin. "I don't want to have our conversation in front of them."

"Then I'll come a couple minutes early." Greg smiled at her. "I'll see you tomorrow." He turned to Debbie. "Ready?"

Debbie nodded and then said her goodbyes to everyone.

She couldn't help but look back as they were leaving. It was obvious Marnie wasn't happy that she and Greg were walking out together.

"I think Marnie has a crush on you," Debbie said to Greg a few minutes later as they walked down the street to Buona Vita.

Greg turned to her. "Marnie?"

Debbie nodded. "You haven't noticed?"

He shook his head. "No. She knows we're just business acquaintances."

"I don't think that's what she's aiming for."

He frowned. "That's awkward. I'll have to make sure I don't give her the wrong idea."

"I haven't seen you encourage her."

"No, but if what you're saying is true, I need to be careful around her." He let out a sigh. "I remember when I started dating Holly— there was this other girl—" He paused and looked down at the ground. "Sorry. Holly's been gone for almost six years now, but the loss steals up on me sometimes, just as raw and fresh as it was the day she died."

"I know what you mean."

"That's right. You lost your fiancé."

Debbie nodded.

Neither one spoke for a heartbeat, and then Greg said, "Sometimes, I think it's too great a risk. Being in love and sharing a life with someone is the greatest gift in the world. But losing them is the hardest thing that can happen. I don't think I'd survive it again."

"I was just thinking the same thing."

He studied Debbie, his blue eyes filled with questions. His voice was gentle when he spoke. "I'm thankful you understand—though I wish you hadn't had to suffer too."

They walked in silence the rest of the way, and Debbie took solace in knowing that she didn't have to explain herself to Greg. He understood.

CHAPTER NINE

The next morning was dark and cold as Debbie entered the warm café. As soon as she turned on the lights, everything felt brighter and happier. There had been many times that she was thankful they had chosen to paint the walls yellow, and this winter, she was especially grateful. No matter how cold it was outside, the café was always cheerful and inviting.

Janet was in the kitchen, clanging pots and pans as Debbie hung up her coat and pulled an apron on. She chose a colorful apron that matched her mood—or, at least, the mood she wanted to have on this dreary day.

"Morning." Janet poked her head into the dining room.

"Good morning."

"I'm taking some pistachio muffins out of the oven, and then I'll be out to chat with you. I have good news."

"Great!" Debbie loved Janet's pistachio muffins—and she liked good news even better.

A couple of minutes later, as Debbie poured herself a cup of coffee, Janet entered the dining room with a tray of assorted muffins. She put them into the bakery case and then asked Debbie, "Do you want one?"

"Yes, please. I'll take a pistachio one."

Janet smiled. "That's what I thought you'd say."

As Janet put two muffins on two plates, Debbie poured her a cup of coffee. They each took a seat at the counter with their breakfast.

"What's the good news?" Debbie asked as she cut open the green muffin. Steam poured out from the center, lifting a fragrant scent into the air.

"I was able to get Polly Pinehurst's married name off the property deed at the recorder's office in New Philadelphia."

Debbie stopped buttering her muffin and looked at Janet. "Yeah?"

"Her married name was Dorset—Polly Dorset."

"That's wonderful! Thank you for doing that. Hopefully, we can find her now." Debbie was about to pull out her phone to put Polly Dorset's name into the search engine, when the café door opened.

Both women looked up to see Harry enter with Crosby.

"Good morning," he said with a grin.

"Good morning, Harry," Debbie replied.

"How are you today?" Janet asked.

"I'm right as rain." His smile was contagious, and Debbie smiled at him in return.

"Hungry?" Janet asked.

"You go on and finish your muffin. Crosby and I can wait for some eggs and toast." He lifted his eyebrows as he took off his hat and coat. "Though I wouldn't mind joining you in a cup of coffee to tide me over."

"Of course." Debbie jumped up and went around the counter to grab a mug and fill it up for their early-morning customer.

Harry took his usual spot on the first stool at the end of the counter, and Crosby curled up under his feet.

"Harry," Debbie said as she set his beverage down in front of him, "I was going to look for you today if you hadn't stopped in."

"Oh?" Harry lifted his cup and took a sip. "How can I be of service to you?"

"We stopped in to visit with Eileen and Ray yesterday, and they told us more about a couple of the young women who Eileen suspected could be the mother of the abandoned baby. One of them was a Polly Pinehurst. We just learned that she married a man with the last name Dorset."

Harry frowned. "I don't remember that much about Polly," he said.

"She was only at the depot for about a week," Janet explained.

Debbie continued. "The other one that Eileen mentioned was Abigail Cobb—"

"I remember Abigail. She was one of the local gals who volunteered at the depot for several years." He shook his head. "I always felt sorry for her."

"Really?" Debbie asked, breaking off a piece of her muffin. "Why?"

"She was a fun, happy-go-lucky kind of gal before the war, but then she left Dennison for a while and came back different. She had aged a lot in the time she was gone, and when she returned, she seemed sad."

"Do you know anything about her personal life?" Debbie asked. "A married name? Anything?"

"I don't think Abigail ever married. After the war, she left Dennison to take a teaching job in another state, if I remember correctly."

"Maybe that's why we haven't found anything about her," Janet said. "We've been looking for Abigail Cobb in Ohio."

Harry rubbed his chin. "I do remember something else about Abigail, though I haven't thought about it in a long time." He shook his head. "Funny how one memory can spark another and another."

"What do you remember?" Debbie asked.

"Abigail had a good friend—you probably remember hearing about her. Mabel Thomas was another local gal. She was sweet on Ray Zink before he left for the war, and she worked at the canteen almost every day."

"I do remember Mabel," Debbie said. "Her daughter attends our church, and we were able to use one of Mabel's old letters to help us find Ray's long-lost sweetheart, Eleanor."

"That's right," Harry said. "Abigail and Mabel were good friends, and Mabel was just as worried about Abigail as the rest of us were. One day, not long after Abigail returned to Dennison from Wisconsin, Mabel told me something about Abigail that I promised to never repeat." He paused. "I guess it probably doesn't matter anymore if I repeat it. Mabel passed on years ago, and I haven't seen or heard from Abigail since she left Dennison."

Debbie forgot about her muffin as she leaned in to hear what Harry had to say.

"Now," Harry continued, "keep in mind that this information came from Mabel, and it was a long time ago, so I might not be remembering it correctly, but I'll try my best."

"Anything you remember will be helpful," Debbie assured him. Just like Eileen's memory of Polly Pinehurst inheriting and then selling her father's farm sparked Ray's suggestion that they look at an old property deed, she hoped that Harry's memory might spark other clues or hints.

Harry took another sip of his coffee and crossed his arms over his chest, as if settling in to tell a good story.

February 21, 1944

Harry worked up a sweat as he loaded luggage onto the passenger train. It was supposed to leave the station in five minutes, and he still had several trunks and suitcases to transfer from the cart to the train. Sometimes he had help, but today, it was all on his shoulders.

Working as fast as he could, he slid the last suitcase into the baggage car just as the conductor yelled "All aboard!" and the steam began to build in the engine.

Thankfully, the winter air cooled Harry as he secured the luggage door and stepped back, wiping the sweat from his brow. He waved at the conductor that he was done and then pushed the cart into the depot, whistling as he walked.

A whole new crew of ladies was working in the canteen. Every day, they came from the surrounding towns. Mothers, sisters, daughters, nieces, aunts, friends, and sweethearts. All of them came to help serve the soldiers going off to war because most of them had already sent their loved ones. It was a way they could contribute to the effort, and it meant more to the men than the women might ever realize.

Harry pushed the cart over to the side of the lobby where it would stay until he needed it again. He glanced into Eileen's office and saw her trying to stay awake at her desk. She didn't complain, but he knew the baby was keeping her up at night. She had her chin in her hand, and her head kept bobbing as she tried to stay alert. He'd heard talk that a family had been found to adopt the baby, but Eileen was still working hard to find the birth mother.

None of it had anything to do with Harry. After finding the baby, he really hadn't had much to do with the investigation. But that didn't mean he wasn't curious or troubled by the whole situation. He kept his eyes and ears open, in case something looked or sounded suspicious. But he left the rest up to Eileen and the police.

The ever-present smell of coffee and baking bread wafted out from the café, making Harry's stomach growl. The volunteers brought new treats every day. Today, he saw that someone had made a cake with chocolate frosting. It had been a long time since he'd had a nice, fluffy piece of cake.

Harry walked into the café and found the chaos he'd come to expect. Today, it was the Port Washington ladies' turn to volunteer in the canteen. They were an efficient group of women, preparing sandwiches for the next troop train.

"Afternoon, Harry," said Mabel Thomas as she greeted him with a smile.

"Afternoon," he said. He hated to come right out and ask for something to eat, since he wasn't a serviceman. Usually, if he stood around long enough, someone would offer him a sandwich.

"Have you had something to eat?" Mabel asked, almost as if she could read his thoughts.

"Not yet." He grinned.

"Here." She handed him a ham sandwich and a cookie. "I was about to take a lunch break. Mind if I join you?"

Harry shook his head. "Of course not."

He'd always liked Mabel. She was a few years older and treated him like a kid brother. She had dark brown hair and bright green eyes and seemed to attract the attention of the passing soldiers. She was currently writing to a serviceman she'd met at the canteen about six months ago. They'd only spent about fifteen minutes together before he left on the train, but they'd exchanged addresses, and she'd been writing to Sam Holman ever since.

"Give me a minute, and I'll get us some milk too," she said.

Harry watched as she maneuvered through the crowd of ladies to the large refrigerator. Abigail Cobb stood close by, her head down, as she made sandwiches. She'd been back in Dennison for a week or so, but Harry hadn't said more than a few words to her.

Mabel stopped by Abigail and put her hand on the girl's shoulder. Abigail didn't look up, but as Mabel spoke to her, Abigail nodded and wiped at her cheeks with her sleeve.

After a few more words, Mabel gave Abigail a side hug and then grabbed a couple of glasses, which she filled with milk, before rejoining Harry.

"Where should we eat?" Mabel asked him.

"Is everything okay with Abigail?"

Mabel glanced at her friend, and Harry didn't miss the telltale worry on Mabel's face. "No."

The answer wasn't what Harry had hoped to hear, but he appreciated Mabel's honesty. "Is there something we can do to help her?"

"I don't think there's anything that anyone can do now."

Mabel led Harry out to the lobby, and they took a seat on the stage in the corner where the band set up for the Friday night dances. A few passengers were waiting in the lobby, and some of the canteen workers bustled in and out of the café, getting ready for the next troop train. No one paid any attention to him and Mabel.

Eileen came out of her office and walked over to the coffee table just as Abigail came out of the café. Harry saw Abigail take one look at Eileen, who hadn't noticed her yet, and turn around and rush back into the kitchen.

Harry frowned as he took a bite of his sandwich.

"Is it just me, or is Abigail avoiding Eileen?" he asked Mabel.

Mabel looked up at Eileen and frowned. "Eileen questioned Abigail about the baby that you found. Thought it was hers."

"If it wasn't hers, then why is she avoiding Eileen?"

Mabel let out a long, low sigh. She bit into her sandwich and chewed on it for a few seconds, as if she was mulling over what she should say about the whole situation.

"Abigail is one of my best friends," she said, quietly, "but I don't know how to help her right now."

"I'd like to help, if I can," Harry said. "You and Abigail can trust me, Mabel."

"I know we can, Harry." She put her sandwich down. "If I tell you, you must promise me you'll never tell anyone else. Abigail would be devastated if she knew I said something, but I can't keep it to myself. I haven't told another living soul about this. I'm at my wit's end and don't know what to say or do to help her. I'm afraid she might do something drastic if she doesn't get help soon."

Harry also put down his sandwich. "Is it really that bad?"

Mabel's face filled with a heaviness that troubled Harry. "It's pretty bad," she said, leaning closer. "Promise me, Harry?"

"I promise. I won't tell anyone else."

Mabel nodded, appearing satisfied with his answer, though she still looked uneasy. "Last spring," she said, "Abigail visited her cousin in Cleveland, and while she was there, she met a soldier who was shipping out that weekend. They spent forty-eight hours together, and right before he left, he proposed to her.

She accepted, and would have married him on the spot, if they'd had time."

Harry could vaguely remember when Abigail had left last spring. He wasn't surprised that she had fallen for someone so quickly. He heard stories about couples eloping all the time—even complete strangers who got caught up in the romance of a soldier leaving for war. He often wondered how many of those couples would be able to make their marriages work once the war was over.

"A couple of months later," Mabel whispered, "after Abigail returned to Dennison, she found out she was going to have a baby."

Harry's eyes opened wide.

"She wrote to her soldier and told him what had happened, but she never got a letter in return."

"Never?" Harry asked.

Mabel shook her head. "Months passed, and Abigail's parents found out. They took her back to Cleveland, to the boy's family, but his parents told them that he died of influenza shortly after he left for boot camp. Abigail was devastated, and her parents were upset, as you can imagine. They didn't even tell the boy's parents that she was pregnant. They didn't want anyone to know."

"I'm sorry to hear all this," Harry said, shaking his head. "I can't imagine how painful it was for all of them."

"Abigail's parents decided to send her to her aunt and uncle. They live on a farm in Somerset, Wisconsin, and they were the only ones who knew who she was. She posed as a young war bride for the townspeople. She stayed with them until she gave birth to the baby, and then came back here."

Harry's eyebrows shot up. "Is she the one who left that baby out there on the platform?"

Mabel shook her head, but she didn't look convinced. "I don't think it was hers, but I honestly don't know. Abigail won't tell me anything else about what happened after her baby was born. I don't know if she left it in Wisconsin or if she brought it back with her."

"If she won't talk about it, then how do you know all this?"

"She told me she was pregnant before she told her parents. And then she wrote to me once she got to Wisconsin. She seemed more open about it before the baby was born, but now she's so sad and won't talk about much of anything." She leaned closer. "She wasn't supposed to write to me while she was away, but she did anyway. She was so lonely. Her aunt and uncle are older and don't have any children. It was a long summer and fall for her."

Harry stared down at his sandwich, wishing he had the words to express his sympathy for Abigail.

Even if he did, he couldn't say anything to her, because he wasn't supposed to know.

"I don't know what to do," Mabel said, shaking her head. "Nothing I say is helping her. I don't think her parents are even talking about it with her. They want to pretend like it didn't happen."

"Maybe she needs to find someone who knows what it's like to go through this kind of pain," Harry suggested. "Someone who is older and wiser. Someone who's had the same experience and can talk to her about it."

Mabel nodded. "That's a good idea. I just don't know of anyone else who has gone through this. No one likes to talk about these things."

Harry knew of someone. "The same thing happened to my sister."

Mabel frowned. "I didn't even know you had a sister."

He nodded. "She's about ten years older than I am. She's married now and lives in Uhrichsville. If Abigail is willing to talk to someone, I think my sister would meet with her—in private. Mira got in trouble in high school and had to go away for a while. No one ever talked about it to me, but I overheard lots of conversations I wasn't supposed to. Mira is a good woman, and she likes to help others. She talks about the hard stuff *better than my mama ever did. I think she'd talk to Abigail."*

Mabel's green eyes lit up with hope. "I think Abigail would be willing. Whenever I talk to her, she says I don't understand—that no one understands. But if I tell her I know of someone who went through something similar, I think she'd agree to meet."

"I'll tell Mira to expect a phone call or a letter—but you don't need to tell Abigail that I know. You can just tell her that you know of Mira through a good friend."

Mabel smiled. "Thanks, Harry. You are a good friend."

Harry returned her smile, happy he could help and wishing that things could be different for Abigail.

"So she did have a baby," Debbie said when Harry finished his story. "Did she ever talk to your sister?"

"She did." Harry nodded. "They became friends, but I never asked Mira or Abigail about it, so I don't know how long they stayed in touch. I think Mira really helped Abigail to heal."

"Somerset, Wisconsin?" Janet asked as she wrote the name of the town on a piece of scratch paper. "And she stayed with her aunt and uncle?"

"That's what I recall," Harry said. "But maybe it was a cousin or something like that. It was family—that much I remember."

"I wonder if their last name was Cobb," Debbie mused.

"Maybe there's still family in the area that might know something," Janet suggested.

"I can call their local historical society and see if they have any information about the Cobb family," Debbie offered. "I'll do that this afternoon."

"What about a birth certificate for a baby born around February of 1944 to Abigail Cobb?" Harry asked.

"We can't get access to a birth certificate without proper authorization," Janet told him. "But we can contact family if we find them."

"That's a good idea." Debbie nodded.

The door opened, and Harry's granddaughter, Patricia, entered. "Hey, Pop Pop!" she said when she saw Harry.

He grinned and patted the stool next to him. "Just in time to eat some breakfast with me."

Debbie finished her muffin. She was happy with the leads they had and eager to check into them.

But first, work.

CHAPTER TEN

During the first lull of the day, just after the breakfast crowd went through, Debbie took a seat at the counter to do some research.

Janet pushed through the kitchen door. "How's the bakery case doing? Does anything need to be refreshed?"

"We could use more glazed donuts, if you have them," Debbie said. "Other than that, everything looks good."

Janet opened the case. "I thought the almond cherry muffins would sell better."

"Not when you make them on pistachio muffin day," Debbie said with a grin.

Janet closed the case and walked over to the counter. "Looking up the Cobb family?"

Debbie swiped to a search engine on her phone. "I'm also going to look up Polly Dorset and see if I can find anything about her."

Janet glanced at her watch and said, "When do we expect Rebekah Potter's granddaughter to arrive?"

"I told her we close the café at two and that we could show her around the depot and museum after that. She said she'd get here about then."

"Great." Janet pulled a coffee mug off the shelf and filled it halfway. "I could use a little caffeine right about now."

Debbie lifted her own mug, which she had just filled, and smiled. "Me too."

After she set it back down, she typed *Abigail Cobb, Somerset, Wisconsin, 1944* into the search engine.

A few ancestry and genealogy links popped up with information about Abigail Cobbs from different generations and places—but not the one Debbie was looking for. She took out *Abigail* and *1944* and just left the last name *Cobb* in the search bar with *Somerset, Wisconsin*. This time, a link appeared from a phone book website.

"It looks like there's a Daniel Cobb in Somerset," Debbie said. She clicked the link. "This says that he's in his forties and lists a few family members in his household."

"If we're lucky, he's related to Abigail in some way."

"There's only one way to find out." Debbie pressed the phone number listed on the webpage.

The phone rang four times, and then it went to voice mail. "This is the Cobb residence, please leave a message," said a male voice.

"Okay," Debbie said, not prepared for that. "This is Debbie Albright. I own the Whistle Stop Café, which is in the Dennison Railroad Depot in Ohio. I'm calling because I'm looking for information about an Abigail Cobb who worked in the depot for the Salvation Army canteen during the 1940s. I'm not sure if you know anything about her, but I was told that Abigail was in Somerset, Wisconsin, for several months in 1944 and that she stayed with family. If you have information about her, could you please give me a call?" Debbie left her phone number and then pressed end.

"Obviously voice mail?" Janet asked.

"Yes." Debbie sighed. "I was hoping for an answer sooner rather than later, but I guess I'll have to wait to see if he calls back."

"We still have Polly Dorset," Janet said.

"I'll try her now." Debbie cleared her search engine and put Polly Dorset's name in place. A few links appeared that had nothing to do with the Polly Dorset they were looking for, but down on the bottom of the page was another phone book link.

"There's a Polly Dorset who lives in Steubenville," Debbie said, her excitement growing. She clicked on the link and saw the most promising information. "And this says she's in her nineties!"

"That has to be her," Janet said. "Is it possible she's still alive?"

"I don't know." Debbie pressed the number. "But I'm going to find out."

Debbie hoped and prayed she wouldn't get sent to voice mail again.

"Hello?" came an elderly woman's voice.

"Hello," Debbie said, trying to contain her enthusiasm. "My name is Debbie Albright. I live in Dennison."

"Dennison," the woman said. "I haven't thought about Dennison in a long time."

"I co-own the Whistle Stop Café in the depot," Debbie continued, "and I'm wondering if you're Polly Pinehurst—the Polly Pinehurst that worked in the canteen for a week or so in 1944."

"Well, I'll be," the woman said, her voice full of wonder. "I sure am!"

Debbie grinned at Janet and gave her a thumbs-up. "I'm so happy I found you, Polly."

"Why on earth would you be looking for me?" she asked. "I was there for a heartbeat. I couldn't have made a lasting impression."

Debbie knew she needed to proceed with caution. If Polly was the abandoned baby's mother, would she want to talk to a complete stranger about it?

"My aunt recently found something in her attic that had been tucked away for a long time," she began. "It was a crate with a baby bottle, a blanket, a cotton sleeper, and a silver rattle inside. There was also a newspaper article from 1944 about a baby that had been abandoned on the depot platform. I was—"

"You think it was mine." It wasn't a question. It was a statement.

"Eileen Turner Palmer gave me your name."

"Is Eileen still alive?" Polly's voice was filled with surprise.

"She is."

"Well, I'll be. I'd like to talk to Eileen. I haven't thought about going back to Dennison since I left there on my wedding day, but I think I'd like to see it again one more time."

"We'd love to have you visit," Debbie said. "There's a museum in the depot, and it has a lot about the canteen days. You might enjoy seeing it."

Polly laughed. "You know you're old when there's a museum about something you lived through. I'd like to come visit you and see Eileen again. Do you think you could arrange that?"

"I'd be happy to arrange a meeting," Debbie said, though she realized that Polly hadn't answered her question. But, then again, she hadn't really asked the question. "Is there anything you can tell me about the baby found on the platform in 1944?"

Polly sighed. "I'll share my story when I come."

Debbie's disappointment returned. She wanted Polly to tell her yes or no or to give her some clue, but she couldn't beg or cajole her to give an answer if she wasn't ready.

After Polly gave Debbie a few dates that might work for her and her friend to travel to Dennison, which was about a fifty-mile drive, Polly said she looked forward to meeting Debbie in person soon.

"That's it?" Janet asked when Debbie ended the call. "She didn't tell you about the baby?"

"No. She was definitely evasive. I guess we'll just have to wait until she comes to Dennison. I'll need to call Eileen and see if there's a day that works for her to meet with Polly here at the depot."

Debbie wasn't happy that she had to wait for Polly's story, but at least she had made some progress. And within a couple of hours, she would meet Rebekah Lehman Potter's granddaughter. Maybe then she'd have all the answers they needed.

Debbie was pushing back the last chair as she swept the floor when she heard a knock on the glass door between the lobby and the café. She glanced up and saw a stylish woman standing on the other side of the door with a smile on her face.

Assuming it was Andrea Stedman, she waved at her and quickly went to open the door. She had put the Closed sign up at two, so Andrea probably assumed the door was locked.

"Sorry I'm late," Andrea said as she extended her hand to shake Debbie's. "I'm Andrea Stedman."

"Hi, Andrea. I'm Debbie Albright. It's nice to meet you."

"It's nice to meet you too." She turned and, for the first time, Debbie noticed two young boys with her. Both had blond hair and blue eyes. The younger one had glasses. "These are my boys, Tucker, who's ten, and Finley, who's eight. I thought it would be fun to show them where their great-grandparents met."

Debbie smiled at the boys. "Hi, guys. Do you like museums?"

Tucker nodded, but the younger one, Finley, just shrugged.

"They got out of school early today to come with me," Andrea said, "so I think they're both liking museums right about now."

Janet entered the dining room from the kitchen. Debbie introduced everyone, and then the five of them walked into the lobby together, toward the museum where Kim was expecting them.

"Harry Franklin was a porter here at the depot during the war years," Debbie said to Andrea. "He told us about your grandparents. And from what he said, he was the one who introduced them to each other, right here in the lobby."

Andrea's eyes lit up as she looked around the room. "This is so neat. Boys, stand there together, so I can get a picture of you where Gram and Granddad met."

The boys obliged, though they didn't seem as excited as their mom.

Debbie was eager to ask Andrea about her grandmother's diary, which she hoped was in Andrea's oversized bag, but she wanted to make sure her guests enjoyed the museum before they talked about the reason Debbie had called her. It could be very upsetting for her.

Soon, they met Kim, and she showed them through the museum, emphasizing the canteen, since it was the reason Rebekah had come to the depot in 1944.

"There's a children's play area," Kim said after they'd spent about forty-five minutes looking at the exhibits and artifacts. She motioned for the boys to follow her.

"This is all so amazing," Andrea said as she scanned the room. "Thank you for reaching out to me. I'm so happy I came." Her eyes lit up. "Oh! I almost forgot. I brought Gram's diary. I skimmed through it again before I came, so hopefully, I can answer whatever questions you might have about her. Are you planning on adding her to the museum?"

Debbie glanced at Janet and then back at Andrea, not wanting to alarm this woman who so clearly admired her grandmother.

"No," she said, gently. "I have a very specific question, actually. And I don't know how to ask it without being blunt."

"Then be blunt," Andrea said with a smile. "Gram was a wide-open book. She talked about her past all the time and wasn't afraid of the truth. She had nothing to hide."

"Okay." Debbie took a deep breath. "The day Rebekah arrived in Dennison, a baby girl was abandoned on the depot platform. The baby was only a few days old, and no one ever stepped forward to claim her."

Andrea's face showed her dismay. "How horrible."

"My aunt might be connected to this story," Debbie said, "so I'm very interested in finding the birth mother. At the time, because

Rebekah arrived on the train that came through right before the baby was found, and because she was a quiet Amish girl, there was some speculation that she might be the mother of the baby."

Andrea's eyes opened wide. "Gram?"

"We don't have any proof," Janet said quickly. "Just what Debbie told you. Rebekah was one of only two known single women on that train, which made her a suspect."

"It couldn't be Gram." Andrea opened her purse and pulled out a blue, cloth-covered diary. "She was brutally honest in her diary— and in life. She said that nothing could ever be hidden from God, so there was no point in hiding it from each other. She also said that no one should ever do anything that needed to be hidden." Andrea talked quickly, as if trying to convince Debbie and Janet. "She was the one who told me that no matter what I did, I could feel comfortable telling her, because she wouldn't judge me. No one is infallible, and everything is forgivable." She opened the book to the first page. "Here. Read this."

Debbie took the diary from Andrea and read the passage out loud.

"'January third, 1943. I hate keeping secrets, so I am starting this diary. There are so many secrets in my family. I cannot trust anyone with my thoughts and feelings except my friend Bethia. So I vow to be brutally honest about everything in this diary, no matter how hard or troubling it might be.'"

"See?" Andrea said. "This was my gram her entire life. She goes on to talk about her struggles in the Amish faith and how she longs to explore the rest of the world. For over a year, she poured her thoughts and feelings into this diary. Her struggles, her doubts, her questions."

"Did she ever talk about a young man in her life?" Janet asked.

Andrea shook her head. "Her parents encouraged her to start courting, but she refused, not wanting to get her heart involved with a man who would ultimately choose to remain Amish. She was starting to think about leaving her community and didn't want to muddy the decision with romance."

"Did she ever mention anything in her diary about being pregnant?" Debbie asked, her hopes slipping through her fingers that they had found the right woman.

Andrea shook her head. "I've read this diary through several times, and there is no mention of anything even remotely related to pregnancy. Gram talked about her life before meeting Granddad in vivid details. If she had been pregnant, she would have written about it."

"Does she say why she came to Dennison?" Janet asked.

Nodding, Andrea took the diary from Debbie and flipped to the second half of the book. "After she married Granddad, she didn't write as often and then stopped completely around the time she had her first child. But she wrote extensively about coming to Dennison."

Andrea handed the diary back to Debbie, who read out loud again.

"'February tenth, 1944. I have made the decision to leave. My parents do not know yet—only Bethia knows, and she is heartbroken. She is the one I struggled to tell the most, because she is my very dearest friend. She has known for a long time that I am not happy here and that I feel God calling me to a different life.

"'I have spent many weeks praying about where I will go, and I believe God wants me to serve in the war effort. My parents will not understand, but I do not need them to. This is something I must do. I can feel it in the marrow of my bones. My destiny is in the Englisch world. I learned about a town called Dennison where there is a Salvation Army canteen. They are looking for volunteers to help. I do not know where I will live or how I will provide for myself, but I believe there will be people there who will help me. And I have God's promises in my heart, telling me this is the right choice.

"'I have always craved adventure, and now I shall have it. I will leave on the train from Wooster on February fourteenth. I can hardly sleep or eat from fear and excitement. I am about to begin a new life, and I can hardly wait.'"

Debbie handed the diary back to Andrea. "If she had been pregnant, I believe she would have said something in her diary. Or been filled with more angst."

"She didn't even mention any boys in here," Andrea said as she closed the book. "She wasn't thinking about romance in the least until she met Granddad, and he swept her off her feet." Andrea smiled. "I don't think she saw him coming—but they were perfect together. Granddad often told me that they were a match made in heaven and that when God stirred Gram's heart to leave her family and church behind, it was because He sent her to him. They didn't spend a single night apart after they were married, and when Gram died, Granddad simply couldn't go on without the other half of his heart. He died in his sleep just a couple weeks later."

"Thank you so much for sharing all of this with us," Debbie said to Andrea. "It definitely answers our questions."

"I think it's safe to say that Rebekah was not the baby's mother," Janet added. "And we can take her off our list."

"I'm happy I could be helpful," Andrea said. "And that this prompted my trip here today. I'm glad I was able to bring the boys to see where our family started."

Debbie was thankful it wasn't a wasted trip, at least for Andrea and her sons. And, like Janet said, they'd eliminated Rebekah from their list, which was helpful.

Hopefully Polly would have answers for them. Or Daniel Cobb. Someone had to know something about the baby.

CHAPTER ELEVEN

The week passed quickly, and the big band dance in Canton was approaching. Debbie was both eager and nervous to spend the evening with Greg. Hearing Andrea's grandparents' story had stirred a lot of emotions and brought back the fear of giving her heart to someone again.

Was it worth the risk?

As she put on mascara Friday evening, just minutes before he was supposed to pick her up, she tried to focus on enjoying their friendship. Because no matter what happened romantically, the truth was she genuinely liked Greg Connor's company. He was funny, kind, thoughtful, and interesting. She loved his perspective and his heart for giving.

Debbie glanced at herself in the mirror. She'd chosen to wear a simple black dress that she'd relegated to the back of her closet when she moved to Dennison. She used to have many occasions to dress up when she lived in Cleveland, but those opportunities were less available now.

She'd put on a pair of black nylons to protect her legs against the cold and would take along a black shawl to wear inside the building, since it might be cool. She paired the dress with silver earrings and a necklace and black heels. Her hair was twisted at the back in a chignon, and she'd curled tendrils around her face. It felt good to dress up again.

After one final look in the mirror, she turned off the light, grabbed her shawl, and walked downstairs to wait for Greg.

Her cell phone rang in the kitchen where she'd left it plugged in. Debbie rushed to answer it before the caller hung up. She'd been expecting a call back from Daniel Cobb all week but hadn't heard a word from him. Either he wasn't related to Abigail, he didn't want to talk to her, or he was out of town and not home to check his messages. Either way, Debbie planned to give him until Monday to return her call, and then she'd try one more time.

When she picked up her phone, she saw it was her aunt calling.

"Hello, Aunt Sherry," Debbie said.

"Hi, Debbie. How are you, dear?"

"I'm good. How about you?"

"I'm okay. I just wanted to call and tell you that your dad agreed to take a DNA test to see if we're blood relatives. In case you didn't know."

Debbie took a seat on her kitchen stool, preparing herself for some big news. "He mentioned it to me. Have you gotten the results back?"

"No. We just sent our samples off today. We should know in a few days if we're biological siblings."

Debbie let out a breath. "Thanks for letting me know."

"I'd like to have you and your parents over for supper the day I get my results. Your dad and I have agreed not to open our emails with the information until we can be together. It shouldn't take long and could happen on Monday or Tuesday, so keep your calendar open."

"Okay. I'd love to be there." Debbie saw headlights flash across her living room and knew that Greg had arrived. "I have plans for this evening, and it looks like my ride's here."

"You go on," she said. "I don't want to keep you from your friends. Have fun. I'll see you soon."

"Okay, goodbye." Debbie pressed the red button to end the call and jumped off the stool to meet Greg at the front door.

He rang the doorbell before she could get there, and when she rounded the corner into the entry, he saw her through the glass window. A big, warm smile was on his face.

Debbie's heart picked up its pace.

She opened the door. "Hi."

"Wow," he said as he openly admired her. "You look beautiful, Debbie."

Her cheeks grew hot, and she was afraid she was blushing. "Thank you. You look good too."

He wore a navy blue peacoat, but she could see a white collar and a tie at his chest. His hair was combed back, and he wore navy blue trousers and black shoes. He did a little turn, a grin on his face. "I clean up pretty nice, don't I?"

If her fluttering pulse was any indication, he cleaned up better than "nice."

She reached for her black wool coat, but he took it from her and said, "Allow me."

Debbie waited as he helped her with her coat. He smelled of aftershave and soap, and when he laid the coat across her shoulders, she felt the feather-like touch of his hands against her neck.

It was almost all she could do not to sigh.

"Ready?" he asked.

"I'll just grab my purse and then I'll be ready. It's in the kitchen."

She was almost happy she'd forgotten it when she'd left the kitchen earlier because it gave her a second to calm her nerves and take a couple of deep breaths. She started to wonder if she'd be able to spend the whole evening with Greg and not let her emotions get the better of her.

Maybe this wasn't a good idea. Maybe she should keep as much space between her and Greg Connor as possible.

As soon as that idea flitted through her mind, she rejected it. She loved spending time with him.

A few seconds later, she was back in the foyer, and he held the door open for her to walk outside. His truck waited in her driveway, still running, no doubt to keep it warm.

The sky was covered with billions of stars, shining brighter than usual in the cold winter air.

They both stopped on the sidewalk and looked up.

"It's a pretty incredible world, isn't it?" Greg asked.

"You know what I love about the stars and rain and snow?"

"What?"

"The world may change around us as each generation comes and goes. But our ancestors looked up at this very same sky and saw the very same stars. Rainstorms, snowstorms, and nature never change. They truly do connect us to the past and the future in ways that nothing else does."

"That's a great thought," Greg said.

Debbie lowered her gaze from the sky and found Greg admiring her again. She smiled, a little embarrassed that she had shared her rambling thoughts, and then they walked to his truck. He held the door open for her and helped her into the warm vehicle.

They had about a forty-five-minute drive to Canton, and just like all the other times she'd spent with Greg, she found it easy to talk to him.

Too easy.

When they arrived at the Onesto, Greg dropped Debbie off at the main doors and promised to be back after he parked his truck.

She entered the front door under a black awning. Dozens of people milled in the entryway, visiting and handing their coats off at the coat check. The building had a plaque that said it was built in 1930, with renovations completed in 2014. It was a magnificent space, with opulent trim work and marble floors. Debbie was eager to explore, since she'd never been there before, but she waited patiently for Greg, who hadn't wanted her to walk in the cold from a nearby parking garage.

Soon, he entered the building, and they smiled at each other.

"I'm excited," he said. "This should be fun." He checked his coat, and they walked through the doors into the main part of the building.

Stunning marble stairs rose ahead of them, and massive crystal chandeliers hung from the two-story ceiling overhead.

"This place is incredible," Debbie said. "I had no idea it was here."

Greg put his hand at the small of Debbie's back as a crowd of people pushed past them.

She felt the light, protective pressure of his hand and loved how it made her feel.

This would be a tough night if she didn't get her feelings under control.

"I believe the ballroom is upstairs," Greg said as he indicated the staircase. "Shall we?"

Debbie walked beside him up the steps, which turned at a landing and split in two directions. They went to the left and were in the upper lobby. Railings allowed them to look down at the main floor where more people entered. Some were dressed in forties attire, while others were in simple cocktail dresses or suitcoats, like Debbie and Greg.

If it hadn't been so noisy from all the conversation, Debbie knew she would hear her heels clicking against the marble floor as they made their way toward the ballroom. The sound of the band floated out into the lobby as they played "Boogie Woogie Bugle Boy," made popular by the Andrews Sisters during WWII.

The ballroom was just as grand and impressive as the rest of the building. The walls were painted a creamy yellow, with white wainscoting, and the floor was a shiny parquet. More crystal chandeliers graced the ceiling. At least three dozen couples were on the dance floor, swinging to the sound of the music, and a hundred more people sat around the tables or mingled near the bar.

"Let's find a table, and then I have a surprise for you," Greg said close to Debbie's ear, above the noise of the band.

"Okay." They found a table with two available seats. Greg pulled out his cell phone and looked at a message and then glanced up and scanned the room. "She said she's wearing a red dress—oh, there she is."

Debbie frowned. "Who's wearing a red dress?"

"It's my surprise for you." Greg took Debbie's hand—whether by instinct or out of excitement, she wasn't sure—and led her through the maze of tables to a woman standing on the edge of the dance floor.

"Greg Connor?" the woman asked him with a smile. She was probably in her late twenties, and she looked physically fit and energetic.

"Yes, and this is my friend, Debbie Albright."

"I'm Paige Rodriguez," she said. She shook Debbie's hand and then Greg's. "Are you ready to dance?"

"Paige is a swing dance instructor," Greg explained to Debbie. "I hired her to teach us a few moves for the fundraiser next week."

Debbie's lips parted. Greg had remembered her comment about needing to learn how to dance?

"Surprise!" he said with a grin, making his dimples shine.

Paige smiled at Debbie, and Debbie smiled back. It warmed her heart to know that Greg had arranged all this for her.

"Thank you," Debbie said to him. "I can't tell you how much this means to me."

"You're welcome. It's my way of saying how much I appreciate all the help you've given us with the fundraiser."

"You didn't need to do that."

"Well." He smiled sheepishly. "It's also because I want to learn too, and I thought we could do it together."

Paige was a great instructor. She spent an hour with them, teaching them the foxtrot, the swing, the samba, and the mambo. Each dance style was unique and took a lot of concentration, but

Greg was a great partner, just as eager as she was to learn, and just as forgiving when she made a mistake.

They laughed their way through Paige's instructions, and when their time with her was up, they said goodbye.

"Want to try one on our own?" Greg asked when the band started another song. Debbie recognized it as "It Don't Mean a Thing," a popular swing song composed by Duke Ellington.

She nodded, and Greg took her into his arms. At first, Debbie was self-conscious and they made a few blunders, but soon, they were laughing and carefree, enjoying the song and the dance.

It was fun to experiment without the teacher looking over her shoulder. Debbie knew she wasn't perfect, and she just had the fundamental steps in place, but it was enough.

Greg's smile lit up the ballroom, and she felt grateful that he was her dancing partner. She wouldn't want to be there with anyone else.

When the song finally ended, they were both winded and Debbie was thirsty.

"Would you like something to drink?" he asked.

"Maybe a soft drink?"

He nodded. "Go rest your feet, and I'll bring one to you."

No one else was sitting at their table, and Debbie was thankful. She liked having Greg all to herself.

Even though her feet hurt, she couldn't keep from tapping her toes to the next song the band played. She'd lost sight of Greg but assumed he had gone to the other side of the room where a bar had been set up. She glanced around at the people who were dancing and then studied the band. She and Greg had come to check it out, though they'd been a little preoccupied.

From everything Debbie saw and heard, the band was a class act. Ten members played classic favorites of the 1940s. They were dressed in black tuxedos, and a band director stood at the front, leading them. The group would be perfect for their fundraiser, and she would tell Greg that very thing as soon as he came back to the table.

It felt like it took Greg forever to return. Debbie had started to wonder if there had been an accident or if something had happened to him, when she saw him moving through the crowd with two glasses in his hands.

Debbie smiled but noticed that he wasn't smiling in return.

And that was when she saw Marnie trailing behind him.

Any shred of fun that Debbie had been having evaporated. Why was Marnie there?

When Greg reached the table, he smiled, but it seemed forced. "Look who I found."

"Hello, Marnie," Debbie said. She rose to greet the newcomer.

"Hi." Marnie gave Debbie a tight smile.

"Here's your soda," Greg said as he handed it to her.

"Thank you."

"Greg tells me you two just took dancing lessons," Marnie said as she eyed Debbie. "I've been taking them for years. I love to dance."

"That's nice." Debbie took a sip of her soda and set it on the table.

The three of them stood in an awkward circle as Marnie kept her gaze on Greg.

He finally seemed to understand what she was hinting at. "Oh— would you like to dance, Marnie?"

"Yes." She took Greg's hand and pulled him away from the table.

Debbie grabbed Greg's soft drink that he held out to her and felt her stomach drop as he walked away.

He gave her an apologetic look. She knew he didn't want to be rude to Marnie.

Debbie sat at the table and had a good view of the dance floor. Marnie was true to her word. She was a good dancer, and she seemed to make Greg a better dancer too. He wasn't stepping on her toes or spinning her in the wrong direction.

When the song ended, Greg looked like he was trying to leave the dance floor, but Marnie cajoled him to stay for another song.

No matter how much Debbie fought it, she couldn't help feeling cast off. She felt bad for Greg, since Marnie had put him in a tough spot, but she also started to get a little impatient with him. He could walk away from Marnie. It might be rude, but wasn't he being rude to leave Debbie all by herself? After all, they had come together.

When the second song ended, Greg finally left the dance floor with Marnie trailing behind.

Debbie's soda was already gone, and she was no longer enjoying the evening. She'd been sitting at the table by herself for twenty minutes.

"I'm sorry," Greg said, searching Debbie's face, no doubt to see if she was angry. "Would you like to dance?"

"No." Debbie shook her head. "I think I'm done dancing for the evening. You can keep on, if you want."

Marnie walked up behind Greg. "Do you need to go home, Debbie?"

Debbie looked at the clock on her phone. "Pretty soon. I have to work in the morning."

"I can always take Greg back with me," Marnie said, "if you want to take his truck home."

Greg frowned. "I brought Debbie, so I'll take her home."

"Oh, come on, Greg," Marnie said. "I just got here, and we dance well together." She put her hand on his arm. "I'd like a little time alone with you."

Debbie had to look away. It was so obvious what Marnie was doing. How could Greg not see it?

"If you want to leave, Debbie, we can go," Greg said, moving away from Marnie's hand. "I'm sorry you came all this way, Marnie, but we've already been here for a while, and I'd like to go too."

Marnie frowned. "Really?"

He nodded as he offered Debbie his hand. She didn't need the assistance to stand, but offering it seemed to come second nature to Greg.

"Goodbye, Marnie," Debbie said as the other woman scowled at her. "I'll see you next week when I stop by to pick up the decorations."

Debbie had ordered bunting and streamers to be sent to the Homes for Humanity office, since it was close to the depot and had a place to store them until they could decorate.

Marnie didn't bother to respond as she walked away from their table.

Greg shook his head as he watched her go. He stood close to Debbie as he lowered her hand.

"I really am sorry about this," he said. "We can still stay and dance for a while if you change your mind. I'll just need to be blunt with Marnie that you're my date this evening and I want to spend time with you."

Even though she knew it wasn't a serious date, Debbie still felt warmed by his words. "Do you want to stay?"

He studied her. "I want to do what you want."

She looked at the dance floor for a moment and then sighed. "I do have to be at work early tomorrow, and we have a forty-five-minute drive home. We should probably head back."

He smiled. "I'm good with that. I'll just stop by and talk with the band director before we leave, and confirm that we'd like them to come play for the fundraiser. That is, if you approve."

She nodded. "I think they'll be perfect for us."

Greg led Debbie to the side of the stage, where he caught the band director's eye. The man came over as the band continued to play, and Greg made his request.

"I'll email the details to you tomorrow," Greg said to him. "Great job tonight."

Soon they were back in the entryway, getting their coats. This time, Debbie didn't wait for Greg to get his truck. She went with him.

CHAPTER TWELVE

D ebbie felt a little sluggish at work the next day. Not only because she was tired, but because she didn't like all the emotions she'd felt the night before—or the ones that were still heavy on her heart this morning.

As she delivered meals, bused tables, and filled coffee cups, her mind was still at the dance with Greg. Despite her best intentions, she was attracted to him, and she didn't want to be. It would be so much easier if she didn't have any feelings for him at all.

"Something on your mind?" Janet asked as Debbie brought a bin of dishes into the kitchen during a lull.

"Why do you ask?" Debbie tried to wipe her face clean of her emotions, but Janet knew her too well.

"You've been pretty distracted all day. I can tell when you're mulling something over."

Debbie sighed as she set the coffee cups into the cleaning rack. "It's kind of silly, actually."

Janet wiped her hands on a towel and then turned from the pot she had been washing and gave Debbie her full attention. "What's going on?"

"You know I went to the dance with Greg last night."

Janet nodded.

Debbie's cheeks were warm. "No matter what I do, I can't help but be attracted to him." She put her face in her hands and leaned against the stainless-steel island.

Janet's giggle could be heard over the noise of the vent hood.

"It isn't funny." Debbie groaned. "It's becoming a problem."

"Why? Greg's a great guy. What's wrong with being attracted to him?"

"Last week, when we went out for pizza, we spoke about losing Holly and Reed. It reminded me how much it hurt to grieve Reed's death, and I don't know if I can risk that again."

Janet was quiet for a moment, and then she said, "Do you think he's attracted to you too?"

Debbie shrugged. "Sometimes. But I suspect he's in the same place I am." She shook her head. "I think he's struggling to decide if it's worth the risk too. And he has his boys to think of."

"And, despite all your reasoning, you're still interested."

"I think he's a wonderful man. And even though we're both feeling cautious, I can't seem to put him out of my mind. Especially after last night. He hired a dance instructor to teach us how to swing dance. And we had such a good time."

"You can still hang out with him. Who knows what'll happen? Maybe down the road you'll both be ready."

"That's what I keep telling myself—but I wish my head would talk to my heart. It would make it a lot easier."

"Is that all that has you distracted?"

Debbie frowned. "No. Marnie Hoskins showed up last night and monopolized Greg's time for two whole dances."

"And?"

"And." Debbie groaned again. "I was jealous, Janet. I haven't been jealous of anyone since high school! I hate that feeling, especially when Greg and I aren't in a relationship."

"Does Greg like her?"

"I don't think so."

"Then what are you worried about?"

"I don't know." Debbie crossed her arms. "I just hate feeling this way. I'm confused and uncertain, and it doesn't feel good."

Janet put her hand on Debbie's arm and smiled. "I know this sounds cliché, but you need to pray about it. Ask God to give you peace as you wait for His leading—in all areas of your life. Whether something develops with Greg later, or if nothing does, ask God to settle your heart. You know that's what you need to do."

It was a beautiful reminder, and one Debbie needed. "Thank you." She gave Janet a hug as the bell over the door jingled in the dining room.

"You're welcome."

Debbie left the kitchen and found Eileen and Kim seating themselves at a table near the counter.

"Good afternoon," Debbie said with a smile. "How are you ladies today?"

"Cold," Kim said with a sigh, "but what else is new?"

Eileen playfully rolled her eyes at her daughter. "Winter comes every year. I don't know why you act so surprised by it."

Laughing, Debbie approached their table. "Would you like to know our special today?"

"We're just here for coffee and pie," Kim said.

"And to share something with you that Kim found and brought to me today." Eileen's eyes shone. "I have more information about Betty."

Betty Harper was a missing piece of the puzzle. The one that Debbie had learned the least about. "I'm so happy to hear that! I'll get your coffee and pie and let Janet know you're here."

"We're in no hurry," Kim said. "If you need to help anyone else."

There were two other occupied tables in the café, but Debbie had already served them their meals, and they were almost done. Ten minutes later, when they'd paid and Janet was able to come out of the kitchen, Debbie took a seat at the table with Eileen and Kim to hear what Eileen had to say. Both she and Janet were ready for a break, so they each hugged a cup of coffee in their hands and waited for Eileen to begin.

"First," Eileen said, "I'm thankful Kim kept searching through my things to see what else she could find."

"I have several of Mom's boxes stored at my house," Kim said. "I knew there was another one with papers and notebooks in it, and I finally found it."

Eileen handed Debbie a yellowed piece of scratch paper that simply said, *Betty Harper, employed by Ernest Hargreaves, Newark, Ohio.*

"It was Hargreaves that rang a bell with me," Eileen explained. "He was a glassmaker in Newark—a very wealthy man. I remember going to his home and being very impressed with the grandeur." She paused a moment. "Now that I think about it, I never met Mr. Hargreaves that day. I only spoke to his daughter." Eileen frowned as she seemed to be searching her memory for the name. "Clair or Clarissa—that's it. Clarissa."

"Why don't you tell us what happened?" Kim suggested. "From the beginning."

Eileen nodded and began her story.

February 28, 1944

The last thing Eileen remembered was looking out the train window as the outskirts of Dennison slipped by. The next thing she knew, she was roused by the porter as he walked down the aisle calling out, "Newark! Next stop, Newark, Ohio!"

Eileen had slept the entire seventy-mile trip, and no wonder. Baby Sarah had been in her care for two weeks and was a colicky infant. Eileen and her neighbor had tried different formulas, but nothing seemed to help. The baby cried from six o'clock to ten o'clock every night, and no matter what Eileen did to soothe her, she didn't want to calm down until she'd worn herself out.

Even now, as Eileen gathered her purse and gloves from the seat next to her, she could hear Sarah's cries in her head.

Thankfully, Eileen's neighbor had agreed to watch the baby on Eileen's one day off that week so she could go to Newark and look for Betty Harper. Eileen had gotten Betty's name and address from the station-master in Newark, and she had decided to come and talk to the woman personally. It was the fastest, easiest way to get the information she needed.

As Eileen descended the train steps onto the platform in Newark, she was surprised at how much larger the depot was than Dennison's. It was a two-story, red-brick building with massive windows trimmed in white. There weren't as many tracks as in Dennison, but there were several that led into and out of the city.

Factories on either side of the depot puffed out smoke and steam, while cars drove by on the frozen street and people rushed in and out of the cold.

Eileen looked at the address she had written on a piece of scratch paper. She wasn't familiar with Newark and didn't know anything about where Betty lived. Was it a rough part of town? An affluent part of town? Did Betty live alone? With her family? With an employer? Would she be shocked to meet Eileen? Embarrassed and insulted that Eileen had come to question her about the abandoned baby?

The questions circled through Eileen's mind as she entered the lobby of the depot. If she knew anything, she knew to start here. She was acquainted with the stationmaster, through phone calls, wires, and letters, though she'd never met him in person.

It didn't take long to locate the office. Eileen knocked on the door, and when a voice said to enter, she did.

"Mr. Marvin Skelton?"

"Yeah?" He looked up from a piece of paper he was writing on and frowned at her. He was an older man, thick around the middle, with white whiskers and hair. "Who might you be?"

"Eileen Turner, from Dennison."

Mr. Skelton's bushy white eyebrows shot up, and he rose from his chair. "Well, I'll be. Come on in, Miss Turner. I wasn't expecting you."

"I made a last-minute decision to come today." She entered his messy office and waited for him to remove a stack of newspapers from a chair before she sat.

"What can I help you with?" he asked.

"I contacted you two weeks ago about a passenger who boarded the train here."

"That's right—I have a note somewhere." He started to move papers around his desk, looking under books and more newspapers, though he couldn't seem to find what he was searching for.

"Her name is Betty Harper," Eileen said. "I have all the information I need about her. I came to Newark

to talk to her, and I was wondering if you're familiar with this address."

She handed him the scrap of paper with Betty's address on it.

Mr. Skelton gave a low whistle. "That's a fancy neighborhood. If Betty lives there, then she's either a very wealthy young woman or a domestic servant. There are no other options."

"Do you know how I might get there?"

"I can drive you myself." He stood and grabbed his hat. "We can talk on the way."

"I couldn't ask you to do that."

"Nonsense. I'm happy to do it." He led her out of the depot and to his car, parked on the street.

As he drove away from the curb, Mr. Skelton said, "What's all this about?"

Eileen wasn't sure how much she wanted to share with this man. She hardly knew him outside of working together and didn't know if he was someone she could trust with the information. But she couldn't just say nothing. It was natural for him to be curious.

"We found a baby abandoned on the depot platform two weeks ago, and we're trying to locate its mother. Betty Harper was one of two single women on the train that day. I would like to know if she saw anything suspicious—"

"Or if she's the mother," he finished for her.

"I'd appreciate it if you kept this information to yourself. I wouldn't want to sully the reputation of an innocent woman. I just need to ask her a few questions."

"I'll wait outside for you," he said. "I don't think you'll be there long."

Mr. Skelton drove away from the factories and into a residential area. The houses grew increasingly larger as they worked their way through the neighborhood until they came to the address Eileen had shown him.

Another low whistle escaped Mr. Skelton's lips as he slowed down in front of the house. "You know whose house this is?"

Eileen shook her head.

"The richest man in town." He nodded at the rambling Victorian mansion with its eaves, gables, and dormers. "That's the house of Ernest Hargreaves. He's a glassmaker. His factory is that gigantic one closest to the depot. His family is one of the oldest in Newark, and he's one of the most powerful men in the county. If Betty Harper lives here, no doubt she's a maid. He only has one daughter, Clarissa."

Eileen couldn't help but be impressed with the information. When Mr. Skelton stopped under the porte cochere, Eileen wasn't sure if she'd have the courage to walk up to the house and ring the doorbell. How would they treat a stranger asking about an abandoned baby?

But that was the reason she had come, so she took a deep breath, lifted her chin, and got out of the car.

"I'll be waiting right here," Mr. Skelton said.

After ringing the doorbell, Eileen stepped back and waited.

It didn't take long for a young woman to answer the door. She wore a black dress with a white apron and a white mobcap. "May I help you?"

"Yes. I'm looking for a woman named Betty Harper. Does she live here?"

"Betty was let go about two weeks ago," the maid said.

Deep disappointment sliced through Eileen. "Do you know where she went?"

The maid shook her head. "She left without warning and didn't leave a forwarding address."

Another young woman, this one in a pretty green dress and black heels, appeared behind the maid. She was very beautiful and had a regal air about her.

"May I help you?" she asked Eileen with a detached tone.

The maid stepped back and dipped her head in deference to the young woman before stepping into the house and disappearing.

"Are you Clarissa Hargreaves?" Eileen asked.

"Yes." Clarissa frowned. "Do I know you?"

"No. I'm here to see Betty Harper."

Clarissa frowned. "Betty? Our maid?"

Eileen nodded. "Do you know where she went?"

Clarissa turned her head and looked over her shoulder then stepped out of the house, pulling the door almost closed behind her. "How do you know Betty?" she asked.

"I don't. I work at the Dennison depot, and Betty was on a train two weeks ago. I need to question her about that trip."

"I'm assuming that was the day Betty was fired. I don't know where she went or how she got there. We haven't heard from her."

"Do you know why she was let go from here?"

"She and my father had an argument. I think she was caught stealing something, but my father won't tell me what happened. He has forbidden me to speak about her. If he hears us now, he'll be very angry." She turned, pushed on the door, and started to walk back into the house, as if dismissing Eileen.

"Please," Eileen said, taking a deep breath. "Was Betty pregnant? Did she have a child?"

Clarissa's eyes opened wide in shock. "No. Betty was with us for years. She was a dependable servant and never gave us any trouble—until two weeks ago."

Eileen sighed. "Are you certain?"

"I would know if my maid was pregnant," Clarissa said as she backed up into the house and started to close the door. "I think you should leave, miss. Betty was not pregnant, and I don't know where she went. Good day."

And, with that, Eileen stood looking at the door.

With a heavy heart, she returned to the car where Mr. Skelton waited.

"No luck?" he asked.

Eileen shook her head. "This was a wasted trip."

She'd hit another dead end. It was time for Baby Sarah to find a permanent home, because Eileen was convinced that they'd never find her mother.

CHAPTER THIRTEEN

hat was it?" Debbie asked, feeling just as disappointed as Eileen sounded.

"That was it." Eileen sighed.

"And you didn't look for Betty after that?" Janet asked.

Eileen shook her head. "I didn't think it would matter. As far as I know, she wasn't pregnant when she left her employment. I didn't think she could have been the mother."

"Unless Clarissa lied for her," Janet suggested. "Or Betty hid the pregnancy well."

Eileen frowned. "I never considered that."

"Hmm." Debbie turned her coffee mug in her hands. "I wonder if Clarissa Hargreaves is still alive. Maybe she'd be more willing to talk about her maid eighty years later."

"It's probably a long shot, but doesn't hurt to find out," Kim said.

Debbie pulled out her cell phone but then paused. "If Clarissa married, we might not be able to locate her."

"The Hargreaves family was very prominent in Newark," Eileen said. "It might be easier to locate Clarissa than you think."

Debbie typed *Clarissa Hargreaves, Newark, Ohio* into her browser.

Almost immediately, her phone was filled with link after link of websites with information about Clarissa.

"It looks like she did marry," Debbie said. She skimmed an article written about Clarissa in 1993. "She married one of her father's business associates, and they eventually took over the glass factory in the 1960s. She was a philanthropist and spent most of her life donating time and money to different organizations."

"That's nice," Eileen said with a smile. "It's always good to hear when people are generous with their money."

"Do any of the websites tell you if she's still alive or not?" Janet asked.

Debbie scrolled through several pages of links then shook her head. "I don't see an obituary."

"That doesn't mean anything," Kim said.

"No, but it gives me hope that she's alive."

Debbie typed Clarissa's married name into a phone book website and was directed to a page listing a Clarissa who was in her 90s, along with her address and phone number.

"According to this," Debbie said as she turned her phone around to let the others see, "she's still alive!"

"What are the odds she'll remember one specific maid?" Janet asked. "We're talking about eighty years ago."

"It doesn't hurt to ask," Eileen said again.

"I'll call her," Debbie offered. She pressed the phone number and waited for someone to pick up.

Finally, there was a young voice on the other end of the phone. "Diamond Willow Assisted Living. How might I direct your call?"

Debbie hadn't prepared herself for an assisted living home—or any other home, for that matter. It took her a second to regroup.

"Hello," she said. "May I be transferred to Clarissa Stewart's room?"

"Mrs. Stewart is not here today," the receptionist said. "She's out with her daughter. May I take a message?"

"Yes. Can you please tell her that Debbie Albright called?"

"Will she know what this is in reference to, Ms. Albright?"

Debbie hesitated. Clarissa would have no idea who Debbie was, even if she told her that she worked at the Dennison depot. More than likely, Clarissa had no connection to the depot, whatsoever, and wouldn't have the faintest idea why a Debbie Albright wanted to talk to her.

"She won't know me," Debbie said. "I own the Whistle Stop Café in Dennison, and her name was provided as someone who might have answers to an old mystery we're trying to solve here. Perhaps I can make a trip to visit with her. I have several questions I'd like to ask, and I think it would be better to do that in person." It would take about an hour and a half to get to Newark, but the sensitive nature of the topic lent itself to an in-person conversation, if possible.

"I'm sure Mrs. Stewart would love a visit from you," the receptionist said. "She has an opening in her schedule this afternoon, before supper. Will that do?"

Debbie's eyebrows shot up. Since when did a receptionist also act as a social secretary to the occupants of an assisted living home? What kind of place was this? Was it for the wealthy and elite only?

"Just a moment," Debbie said. She put her hand over the mouthpiece of the phone to look at Janet. "Could you drive with me to Newark to meet Clarissa this afternoon?"

Janet nodded. "Sure."

Debbie spoke to the receptionist again. "We can be there about four o'clock."

"Perfect. Mrs. Stewart will be expecting you."

"Thank you." Debbie ended the call. "That was interesting."

"A pretty posh retirement home?" Kim asked.

"That's what it sounds like."

"I'm excited to meet her," Janet said. "I hope she remembers Betty and that this isn't a wasted trip."

No trip was wasted if it offered answers or more clues.

Debbie hoped for both of those things when they met with Clarissa Hargreaves Stewart.

A couple of hours later, Debbie was in the driver's seat with Janet beside her as they navigated through Newark. Debbie had put the address of Diamond Willow into her car's GPS and followed directions to the property where Clarissa Stewart lived.

"I wonder if she'll even remember Betty Harper," Janet said as they passed through a tree-lined street with beautiful Victorian homes gracing either side. Large wraparound porches, turrets, gables, and bric-a-brac decorated many of the houses.

"We can hope," Debbie said as the GPS told her to take a right. "Maybe she knows more than we think."

"I like your optimistic attitude."

"I have to be optimistic. If it turns out that my aunt is the baby who was abandoned on the depot platform, then I'm going to be even more determined to find her birth mother. If Clarissa doesn't have any answers, maybe she can point us to someone who does."

The GPS said they were getting close. And when it finally said they had arrived, Debbie stared at the home in awe. It was easily the largest house in the neighborhood—perhaps even the whole town. A beautiful porte cochere sat to the side, while a massive front door faced the road. The house was made of large red stone and appeared almost gothic. An ornate sign on the front lawn said DIAMOND WILLOW ASSISTED LIVING.

Debbie turned in to the driveway and found a place to park in the small lot. The grounds, though covered in snow, were expansive. Manicured hedges and bushes suggested that the gardens would be lavish and beautiful in the summer.

"Ready?" Debbie asked.

Janet nodded, and they both exited the car. When they reached the front door, Debbie tried to open it but realized it was locked.

"Maybe we have to ring the doorbell," Janet suggested.

Debbie did, and a voice came from the intercom near the doorbell.

"Yes?"

"Hello," Debbie said, leaning forward. "My name is Debbie Albright. I have an appointment with Mrs. Stewart at four o'clock."

"Please come in." The door clicked, and Janet pulled it open.

A small entry had five steps that led up to a hallway. The woodwork was dark and heavy, the carpet runners were thick, and everything looked opulent. A receptionist sat at a beautiful mahogany desk and smiled as the ladies approached. A fresh bouquet of red roses decorated the desk.

"Hello," the receptionist said.

"Hi," Debbie said. "I'm Debbie Albright, and this is my friend, Janet Shaw. We're here to see Mrs. Stewart."

"Yes. Mrs. Stewart is expecting you. I'll take you to her rooms. We have an elevator, if you'd like to take it upstairs."

"I'm fine," Debbie said, looking at Janet to see if she would like to use it. Janet shook her head.

The receptionist motioned for them to follow her.

"Do you know Mrs. Stewart?" the receptionist asked.

"No," Debbie said. "We haven't met her."

"Her daughter, Katharine, is visiting today. She'll be happy to meet you."

They went up the winding stairs to the second floor. All the wood was just as dark and heavy on this level, and several tall doors flanked either side of the hallway with beautiful, gilt-framed paintings between them.

"The original owner of the home was an art collector," the receptionist said as she noticed Debbie admiring some of the medieval paintings. "Most of these are authentic and very valuable."

Debbie lifted her eyebrows, duly impressed.

The receptionist stopped and knocked lightly on a door. "Mrs. Stewart, you have guests."

The door opened, and a woman who looked to be in her mid-to-upper sixties appeared. She had a pleasant, if curious, smile on her face.

"Katharine, this is Debbie Albright and her friend, Janet Shaw. They've come to see your mother."

"Thank you, Roseanna," Katharine said to the receptionist.

Roseanna turned and headed for the stairs.

"Hello," Debbie said, extending her hand to Katharine. "I'm Debbie, and this is Janet."

"I'm Katharine Stewart Crawford," she said. "Won't you come in?"

They entered the room, and Debbie was just as impressed as she had been with the rest of the house. The area was large and set up like a parlor or living room with ornate furniture and thick plants.

"My mother is freshening up in her bedroom," Katharine said. "Please have a seat."

Debbie and Janet sat together on a floral-covered sofa with claw feet.

"Would you like something to drink?" Katharine asked. "I can have something sent up."

"No, thank you," Debbie and Janet said at the same time.

Katharine took a seat on one of the wingback chairs. She moved with grace and elegance, completely at home in this lavish environment.

"This home is lovely," Debbie said.

"My grandfather built it." Katharine smiled as she looked around the room. "My mother inherited it after his death, and I was raised here with my younger brother. As Mother aged, though, we realized it was too much for her to keep up. My brother and I were not able to take it on, so we opened it up to three other residents, all Mother's friends, and turned it into an assisted living home. It has been wonderful for Mother, who didn't have to leave the house she's lived in all her life."

"This was the Hargreaves home?" Debbie asked, a little surprised. This was the house Eileen had come to all those years ago.

"Yes." Katharine nodded. "Are you familiar with my family's history?"

"Just a little bit. I know your grandfather was a glassmaker."

"That's right." Katharine turned at the sound of a door opening.

An elderly woman entered. She wasn't stooped or bent over, and her eyes were clear and keen. She walked with a steady gait to the sitting area while Katharine, Debbie, and Janet rose to greet her.

"Mother, these ladies have come to meet with you," Katharine said. "This is Debbie Albright."

Debbie leaned forward and shook Mrs. Stewart's hand. "It's a pleasure to meet you, Mrs. Stewart."

Mrs. Stewart nodded.

"And this is Janet Shaw," Katharine continued.

"It's nice to meet you," Janet said, as she too shook Mrs. Stewart's hand.

"Won't you have a seat?" Mrs. Stewart said in a gentle, even voice. "Katharine, ring for tea, please."

Katharine lifted a cell phone. She typed something and then set it back on the table.

Mrs. Stewart frowned. "I miss the days when we simply tugged on the bellpull and the maids came running."

"You know it's more convenient to send a text to the kitchen," Katharine said with a shake of her head.

The four of them faced each other. Mrs. Stewart sat straight, with perfect posture.

"Now, tell me what this is about," she said. "Are you here to ask for a monetary donation?"

Debbie's mouth opened in surprise. "No." She swallowed, suddenly feeling a little intimidated by this woman. "Janet and I own a café in the Dennison depot, and someone came to us recently to look for answers about a baby that was abandoned on the train platform in 1944."

Debbie watched both Mrs. Stewart's and Katharine's expressions to see what they might give away about this topic. Neither woman did more than blink.

"Why have you come here?" Mrs. Stewart asked. "What does that have to do with me?"

"In the initial investigation," Debbie continued, "it was discovered that a woman by the name of Betty Harper was on the train that came through Dennison around the time the baby was left. She was traced back to this residence, but she had been fired from her job as a maid here."

"The stationmaster at the time, Eileen Turner, came to ask about her," Janet added. "She said she met you, but you didn't know where Betty had gone."

"I remember Miss Turner's visit, though I didn't know her name until now," Mrs. Stewart said. "I also remember Betty, but I'm afraid your coming here today is wasted. I never heard from Betty again. I don't know where she went, or why she was fired."

Deep disappointment pinched at Debbie. "Do you recall anything about her that might be helpful?"

Mrs. Stewart shook her head. "I'm afraid not. She wasn't with us long, and I hardly spoke to her."

Something Eileen had said earlier struck Debbie and made her question Mrs. Stewart's response. "Eileen said that you told her Betty had been with you for years."

The first flicker of discomfort shifted across the elderly woman's stoic face. "This was eighty-some years ago. How am I to remember every little detail? All I know is that Betty Harper was not noticeably pregnant. I would have known if my maid was expecting a child."

Katharine listened intently to the conversation but added nothing. When the tea came, Debbie and Janet sat awkwardly, trying to fill the time with small talk. It was clear Mrs. Stewart didn't know anything about Betty—or, if she did, she wasn't going to share.

When they finished their tea, Debbie and Janet rose to leave.

"I'll see you out," Katharine said.

"Thank you for your time," Debbie said to Mrs. Stewart. "If you happen to remember anything important, please let us know."

"Why are you looking for the baby's mother now? All these years later?" Mrs. Stewart watched Debbie closely for her answer.

Should she tell her about Aunt Sherry? What would it hurt?

"My aunt discovered a crate in her garage with the items that came with the baby. She has reason to believe she might be the child, and I'm determined to help her find out."

"Your aunt?"

Debbie nodded.

Mrs. Stewart offered a smile that seemed more practiced than sincere. "I'm sorry I cannot help you find what you're looking for."

Debbie thanked her, and they said their goodbyes.

Katharine walked with Debbie and Janet through the upper hallway, down the stairs, and to the door.

As Debbie turned to say goodbye, Katharine spoke in a quiet voice. "My mother used to get letters from a woman named Betty Harper when I was younger. She wrote to Mother for decades. I once asked her who Betty was, and Mother told me she was a friend from a long time ago. I never questioned her beyond that."

Debbie glanced at Janet, who looked as surprised as Debbie felt.

"I don't know why Mother is lying," Katharine said. "But I cannot abide lies—my father was a liar, and he dismantled my world as a teenager. I can't let my mother lie as well, no matter who she is trying to protect."

Katharine took a deep breath. "Mother has saved all of her family's correspondence in the attic. I'll see if I can find those letters, and, if Mother agrees, I'll let you know whether or not I discover something important."

"Thank you." Debbie smiled at Katharine. "We appreciate any help you can give us."

As Debbie and Janet pulled out of the parking lot and headed home, Debbie felt a newfound surge of hope. Perhaps there would be something in Betty Harper's letters that would help them learn the truth about Baby Sarah.

CHAPTER FOURTEEN

ebbie stood in her kitchen on Tuesday afternoon, measuring flour into a mixing bowl and thinking about her aunt Sherry. She was making a chocolate cake to take to Aunt Sherry's house for dessert that night. After the cake baked and cooled, she'd smother it with sweetened condensed milk, caramel, whipped cream, and toffee candy crumbled over the top. It was her father's favorite dessert. No matter what their answers were to the DNA test, it would be an emotional night. She wanted to sweeten it as much as possible.

The oven dinged, telling Debbie that it was preheated. She quickly finished combining the wet and dry ingredients for the cake and then poured the batter into the prepared pan.

Her thoughts swung between the DNA test results that would be revealed that night and the ongoing search for Baby Sarah's mother. The only person who had been ruled out was Rebekah Lehman Potter. That left Polly Pinehurst Dorset, Betty Harper, and Abigail Cobb. Polly was coming to the café the next day and would hopefully have some answers for Debbie, but they still hadn't heard from Daniel Cobb in Wisconsin.

After Debbie set the timer, she went to her purse hanging by the back door and pulled out her cell phone. She would leave one more message with Daniel Cobb, and if he didn't return her call, she would consider it a dead end.

She found his number in her recent calls, pressed the talk icon, and walked into the living room to take a seat on the sofa.

The phone rang twice, and then a man answered. "Hello?"

Debbie sat up straighter. "Hello. My name is Debbie Albright. I called last week and left a message. Is this Daniel Cobb?"

"Yes." There was a pause, and then he said, "I didn't get the message. Sorry. What is this about? Are you trying to sell me something?"

"No." Debbie stood and started to pace. "I live in Dennison, Ohio, and I own the Whistle Stop Café, which is in the railroad depot. A couple of weeks ago, my aunt brought me something she found in her attic, and since it was connected to the history of the depot, she asked for my help trying to figure out where it came from."

"Okay," he said slowly, as if he followed her so far but didn't see how this applied to him.

"She brought me a crate with a baby blanket and a few other items inside. There was also a newspaper from February fourteenth, 1944, with a story about a baby that was abandoned on the depot platform that day. The baby's birth mother was never found, but there were four young women who were considered possible suspects, for lack of a better word."

"Okay," he said again.

Debbie took a deep breath. "One of those women was Abigail Cobb. She was from Dennison but went to live with her aunt and uncle for several months in Somerset. We know she was pregnant and that her fiancé was a soldier who died in boot camp. She was sent away to have the baby, but we don't know if she left the baby in Wisconsin, or if she brought it back to Dennison and left it on the platform."

"Why would she do that?" he asked.

"Perhaps she wanted the baby to be adopted by someone in Ohio so she could keep her eye on her over the years."

"I guess that's plausible."

"Mr. Cobb, I'm wondering if you know anything about Abigail Cobb. Since you're the only person in Somerset with that same last name, I'm hoping you might be able to shed some light on this story. Perhaps you're related to the same family?"

He was quiet for a moment, and then he said, "I actually do know of Abigail Cobb, and I'd be happy to tell you about her."

Debbie paused in her pacing. Was she about to learn something important? Something that might be able to help them solve this mystery?

"What can you tell me?" she asked.

"My father told me this story many years ago, just before he died. I don't know if he was trying to clear the air, or if he simply wanted me to know the truth. I honestly didn't think it would ever matter—not really. I've been curious about a few things, but it doesn't change my life in any way."

Debbie held her breath, waiting patiently.

"My father's name was Harold Cobb. I never met his parents, because they both died before I was born. They were a farming couple, well into their fifties when Dad was born. They were excited to have a son to carry on the name and take over the farm one day. I still own the farm and hope to give it to one of my children when I'm ready to retire."

"Were they related to Abigail?"

"Yes." Mr. Cobb let out a sigh. "Abigail was their niece. My father told me that Abigail came to their farm pregnant. Her fiancé had died, just as you said, but her parents didn't want the situation to ruin her life. After the baby was born, Abigail returned to Dennison and tried to pick up the pieces of her broken heart."

"That's the story I've been told too."

"My father, Harold, was Abigail's baby. He was born on February tenth, 1944. She didn't want to leave him, but she had no choice. As soon as she was able to travel, she was put back on a train and returned to her parents. My grandparents adopted the baby and raised him as their own. Abigail exchanged letters with my grandparents until my grandmother's death. I have her letters, which my father gave me before he died." There was another pause. "I'm sorry I can't help you, but Abigail was not the woman who left a baby girl on the depot platform in 1944."

Debbie let out her breath. "Thank you for telling me her story. I'm disappointed that I still don't know the birth mother's identity, but I'm thankful to know what happened to Abigail's baby."

"I can't imagine what Abigail went through, giving up her child," Mr. Cobb continued. "It's my understanding that she never married, and became a schoolteacher."

"That's what I've been told as well."

"I'm grateful to Abigail," Mr. Cobb said. "She sacrificed a lot to bring my father into the world, even though she had to leave him with her aunt and uncle. My grandparents loved my father very much. He brought them great joy and happiness, especially in their older years, and he loved them too. I wouldn't be here, and neither would my children, if it wasn't for Abigail."

Debbie smiled. "Thank you, again, for sharing with me today."

"You're welcome. If there's anything else I can help you with, don't hesitate to call me back. I'm sorry I didn't get your first message."

"That's okay. I'm just happy I was able to connect with you today. Goodbye, Mr. Cobb."

"Goodbye."

Debbie ended the call and stood for a long time, looking out the front window at her yard. It was a little warmer today, but the world was still covered in snow.

Daniel Cobb's words circled around in her mind, both comforting her and making her sad for a young woman whose heart had broken eighty years ago. And then to be questioned by Eileen—and the police—so soon after her arrival back home must have been devastating. No wonder Abigail was distraught when she was in Eileen's office that first day. She'd lost the man she loved and had been forced to give up their baby. Her body and soul were trying to heal from trauma when she was questioned. It probably ripped her wounds open all over again. Not to mention, she had very few people to talk to about it.

Debbie hoped and prayed that Abigail had found some sort of peace over the years. She took comfort in knowing that Harry's sister had become Abigail's friend. It was also nice to know that Abigail's aunt had written to her about her son. Perhaps even sent pictures of him.

It was little consolation, but it eased Debbie's sadness for a woman she would never meet.

And it took one more person off their list. Neither Deborah nor Abigail was Baby Sarah's birth mother.

But who was? And, more importantly, was Aunt Sherry Baby Sarah?

At five o'clock on the dot, Debbie drove up to her aunt's house. Aunt Sherry lived in a bungalow, not much different than Debbie's house, on the outskirts of town. Aunt Sherry had purchased it from her parents when they were ready to downsize and move into an apartment after Debbie's dad went to college.

Debbie loved going to Aunt Sherry's house when she was little. Her dad told her stories about being a boy there and had shown her where he had written his name on the inside of a closet door as a child, his favorite climbing tree, and the window he'd broken with a baseball when he was a teenager.

Another car pulled into the driveway. It was her mom and dad. Debbie waved at them but instantly knew her dad wasn't doing well. He looked pale and nervous. When he waved back, it was a half-hearted attempt at a greeting, but Debbie couldn't blame him. She would be a wreck right now if she were in his shoes.

"Hello," Debbie's mom called as she got out of the car.

"Hi." Debbie was holding her cake pan, so she couldn't give her parents a hug. "How are you feeling, Dad?"

He sighed. "I got an email with my results in an attachment last night, like Sherry. It's been hard not to look at them."

"I bet."

The front door of Aunt Sherry's house opened just as they reached it. "Here you are," Aunt Sherry said. She smiled, though Debbie could see the strain in her eyes.

"Hey, Aunt Sherry." Debbie entered the house first. Her aunt was a saver and tended to hold on to things that others might get rid of or send to the dump. Newspapers and magazines were stacked in her covered porch, and boxes were piled on an old couch. It was a wonder that she hoped to get the house up for sale soon. There was a lot of work left to be done.

"Come on in and make yourselves at home," Aunt Sherry said. "Supper's on the table."

"It smells good," Debbie said, trying to keep everything as normal as possible. "What did you make?"

"Dumplings, sausage, and sauerkraut. Your dad's favorite."

It seemed they were all trying to make this easier on Dad.

Dad gave Aunt Sherry a hug—one that lasted longer than Debbie would expect. Mom looked at Debbie over Dad's shoulder and lifted her eyebrows.

"I love you, Sherry," he said.

"I love you too, Vance." Aunt Sherry patted his shoulder and pulled out of the hug. She gazed at him for a few heartbeats before she said, "We're going to be okay. No matter what the results say. At the end of the day, we're family, and nothing can change that."

Dad nodded and took a deep breath before he stepped back from his sister.

The dining room was just as crowded as the rest of Aunt Sherry's house. She loved knickknacks, doilies, and mementos from travels, and they were proudly displayed in a curio cabinet, on the hutch, and on shelves that were hung on the walls.

"Where would you like the cake?" Debbie asked.

"Just set it on the table. I have a cake server ready for you."

Mom had brought a salad, and it was ready to go, so she set it on the table as well.

"I'll take your coats." Aunt Sherry waited as they took off their coats and handed them to her. "I'll be right back."

She left the dining room, and Debbie took a seat across from her parents. They sat at the table that her grandparents had purchased when they were first married. Debbie thought about all the gatherings that had taken place there. Did her grandparents ever think that their children would one day come together to find out from a DNA test if they were biologically related? Would they be appalled right now? Laughing? Or very serious, knowing that two of their children were about to learn a secret that they had kept hidden?

No one said a word while Aunt Sherry hung up their coats in the other room. Dad stared at the plate in front of him, and Mom glanced between Debbie and Dad with concern in her eyes.

When Aunt Sherry came back into the room, she said, "I don't know why everyone's acting so serious. Either I'm adopted or I'm not. Whether or not we know about it won't change the truth."

Debbie smiled at her aunt. Dad finally looked up from his plate.

"Should we eat first or check the test results first?" Aunt Sherry asked Dad.

"I don't think I could eat a thing right now," Dad said. "Let's look at the results."

"Okay. Do you have your phone? The woman I spoke to said she would send the same thing to both of us, so it doesn't pay for me to grab my computer if you can access her email from your phone."

"I have it here." Dad pulled his phone out of his back pocket and laid it on the table.

Aunt Sherry took a seat.

"What will the results tell you?" Debbie asked.

"Whether or not we're biologically related," Aunt Sherry said. "But that's about it."

"So, if you were adopted," Debbie clarified, "it wouldn't tell you who your blood relatives were?"

"Not this test. That would be a whole different test, and I'd have to find a possible relative to see if we shared the same DNA."

Debbie nodded.

"Here we go." Dad picked up his cell phone and swiped it a few times.

Debbie held her breath again.

Dad tapped the screen, and everyone watched as he read the results.

"Well?" Aunt Sherry asked, leaning forward.

The look on Dad's face was hard to read. He was devoid of emotion when he finally glanced up at his sister.

"We're not biological siblings," he said in a hushed, stunned voice.

Aunt Sherry's mouth opened, and she stared at him. Despite her almost indifferent attitude earlier, the news seemed to affect her deeply.

"We're not?" she said in an equally quiet voice.

Dad shook his head as he handed his phone to her. He was trembling, and he looked like he was going to be sick.

Aunt Sherry took the phone and stared down at the screen. She put her hand to her mouth, and tears began to run down her cheeks. "I hoped it wasn't true."

Mom was busy comforting Dad, so Debbie stood and went to her aunt. She put her hand on Aunt Sherry's shoulder, not knowing what to say.

"How could Mom and Dad have lied to us?" Dad asked. "Why didn't they tell us the truth?"

"I'm sure they had their reasons," Mom said. "It was a different time. People were more private back then."

"What if they were ashamed of me?" Aunt Sherry asked. "Especially if I was the baby abandoned at the depot. Were they embarrassed to tell everyone that their daughter was the unwanted child someone rejected?"

"Of course they weren't," Debbie said, thinking of Abigail Cobb wanting her baby so badly. "And your birth mother probably had no choice. You were wanted, but her circumstances wouldn't allow her to keep you. Maybe she fell in love with a soldier who died or was shipped overseas before they could be married, and she panicked. Anything could have happened. I'm sure she mourned her loss her entire life."

Mom nodded. "Debbie's right, Sherry. You were not only wanted by your birth mother, but you were very much wanted by your adopted parents. They chose to let you believe you were their biological child so you wouldn't feel rejected. We need to trust that they had their reasons and not blame them, especially when they're not here to defend themselves."

Aunt Sherry set Dad's cell phone down and put her face in her hands. She took several deep breaths and then looked up at them. "I'm not going to pretend like this won't take some getting used to. I may never adjust to the news. But I can't cry about it forever." She wiped at her cheeks and sniffed. "Let's eat before the food gets cold, and then we'll enjoy our dessert and coffee. I'm sure we'll have a lot to say over the next few months, and we don't need to try and say it all now."

Debbie returned to her seat and glanced at Mom. They shared a concerned look, but they needed to consider Aunt Sherry's and Dad's feelings. If Aunt Sherry didn't want to discuss it right now, then they wouldn't.

"When you're ready to talk," Debbie said to her aunt, "we'll be here."

Aunt Sherry smiled at her. "I appreciate that, honey."

Debbie wasn't sure if her dad would be able to eat. He still looked like he was ill.

Finally, he reached for his phone and put it back into his pocket. Aunt Sherry said, "Vance, you say grace."

Dad reached for Aunt Sherry's hand and then for Mom's. Mom took Debbie's hand, and Debbie took Aunt Sherry's.

They all bowed their heads, and Dad said, "Lord, we thank You for this day, for this food, and for this family. No matter how we were put together, it wasn't an accident on Your part. You created Sherry to be a part of our family, just as You created me, and Becca, and Debbie. We thank You for that, and ask You to bless us as we move forward. Amen."

"Amen," everyone echoed.

Aunt Sherry held Dad's hand a moment longer before she let him go, and they smiled at each other.

It wasn't going to be easy to navigate this new information, but Debbie was certain they would come out stronger for it.

And she was more determined than ever to find Aunt Sherry's birth mother.

Because she knew, without a doubt, that Aunt Sherry was Baby Sarah.

CHAPTER FIFTEEN

*D*ebbie was still shaken up and distracted about Aunt Sherry's news the next day as she got ready for work. The sun had not yet come over the horizon, and her house felt colder than usual in the darkness of a winter morning. She took a shower and then dressed in jeans and a red sweater in honor of Valentine's Day.

She couldn't stop thinking about Aunt Sherry. It was mind-boggling that after all these years they learned that Aunt Sherry was adopted. If Debbie's grandparents hadn't saved the crate and baby blanket, would her aunt have ever suspected? Had they secretly wanted Aunt Sherry to find out someday? Maybe that was why they'd saved the items.

But then those questions prompted others. Did Debbie's grandparents know the birth mother? Or were they just as clueless as everyone else about who she was?

Debbie thought through the last two remaining suspects. Polly and Betty. What if their involvement turned out to be dead ends? Then what? Would Aunt Sherry ever know the truth? Perhaps she could do DNA testing through a couple of genealogy sites and try to figure out who some of her relatives were. That might help them narrow it down, but it seemed like a long shot.

Maybe Debbie was missing a clue. There had to be something more.

As she blow-dried and styled her hair, she thought about the crate and the things that were inside. She hadn't really studied any of the items. Maybe she needed to take a closer look.

After she finished getting ready, she turned off the lights and went downstairs to the coat closet in her entryway where she had put the crate.

It was so small. Debbie could hardly believe a baby fit inside it—that Aunt Sherry had fit inside it.

She went into the living room and set it on the coffee table before taking a seat on the sofa. She should really get to the café, but she had a couple more minutes to spare.

Gently, she took the newspaper, the moth-eaten blanket, and the cotton sleeper out of the crate. She looked each one over carefully, trying to see if there were any hidden messages or clues, but found none. At the bottom of the crate were the baby bottle and the silver rattle. There was nothing remarkable about the bottle. It was clear glass with a rubber nipple that had cracked from old age.

Debbie lifted the rattle out and shook it. The sound was still clear, though the silver was tarnished. It had a round, flat head, and an ornately decorated handle with two engraved letters, though they were hard to make out because of the deep tarnish and buildup of grime. Debbie grabbed a tissue from the box on the coffee table and cleaned the handle as best she could. She was able to make out the letters *BH*.

Did that stand for Betty Harper? Had this rattle been hers before it was given to Aunt Sherry? Debbie decided that when she came home from work, she would use a tarnish remover to clean up the rattle. From what she could tell, underneath the tarnish and accumulated dirt, it was in almost perfect condition. At least it was something that Aunt Sherry could have from her birth mother.

Debbie put everything back in the crate and left it on the coffee table. She went to the kitchen and pulled on her coat. She found her purse and cell phone and then left the house.

She was still thinking about the initials on the rattle when she drove up to the depot. It was dark, though the sky was starting to lighten in the east.

As Debbie went about her morning chores in the café, she shifted her thoughts to Polly Dorset, who was supposed to stop by that afternoon. Debbie had found a time that Eileen could join them, and Kim would pick her mother up from Good Shepherd around one thirty. They would meet at the café at closing time so they could have a little peace and quiet to visit.

What would Polly have to say? Would she shed light on the story? Could she be the mother and the initials on the rattle be from something else? It seemed like anything was possible.

The day seemed to crawl as customers came and went. Harry stopped in for his usual morning coffee and breakfast. Debbie wasn't ready to tell him about Aunt Sherry. She hadn't asked her aunt if she could share the news, so she needed to keep it to herself.

Finally, it was two o'clock. Debbie had already wiped the counter and cleaned the glass on the bakery cabinet and was just about finished with her sweeping when the bell over the door jingled. She looked up and saw Eileen and Kim enter the café.

"Are we on time?" Eileen asked.

"Right on time," Debbie assured her. "Happy Valentine's Day."

"To you too. Haven't heard from Polly yet?"

Debbie shook her head. "She didn't call to cancel, so hopefully she didn't forget about us." She grabbed the dustpan and swept the dirt into it, then she dumped the contents in the garbage and put the broom back. "I still have the coffee on. Would you like a cup?"

Both women nodded as Janet exited the kitchen. "Hello," she said.

"Hello, honey," Eileen said.

"No word from Polly yet?" Janet asked Debbie.

"Not yet."

Janet reached for a plate and filled it with several treats from the bakery case. She brought them over to the table where Kim and Eileen sat. Debbie was right behind her with the coffee.

For the next ten minutes they drank their coffee and made small talk.

Debbie kept glancing at the clock, feeling more and more disappointed with each passing minute. Finally, she said, "Maybe I should try to call her. Make sure everything's okay."

"Might be a good idea," Janet agreed.

But when Debbie rose to get her phone, she saw two women entering the depot lobby.

One was tall, though stooped with age, and the other was short and much younger.

"It looks like they're here." Debbie went to the café door and opened it for the women. "Hello. Welcome to the Whistle Stop Café. You must be Polly Dorset?"

The taller woman smiled. "That's me. Goodness, it's strange to be back here after all these years. It hasn't changed much."

Debbie shook Polly's hand. "I'm happy to welcome you to our café."

"This is my neighbor, Gail," Polly said. "She offered to bring me, since I don't do much driving anymore."

"It's nice to meet you, Gail," Debbie said as she shook Gail's hand. "Won't you come in?"

The newcomers entered the café, and Janet and Kim rose from the table to greet their guests. Eileen stayed seated, since it wasn't as easy for her to get up and down.

Introductions were made, and then Polly faced Eileen and smiled.

"It's been a long time, Miss Turner," she said.

"Mrs. Palmer now," Eileen responded with a smile. "I'm a widow."

"Same here," Polly said. She settled in the chair next to Eileen, and the two women looked at each other for a few moments.

"There aren't many of us left," Polly said. "The Greatest Generation is almost a thing of the past."

Eileen took Polly's hand and squeezed it. "But we had a good run, didn't we?"

Debbie brought coffee for Polly and Gail, and took her seat again.

Eileen and Polly talked for a few minutes about the canteen and the war years while the others listened with rapt attention. Eventually, Eileen came to the reason for Polly's visit.

"Debbie said that you wanted me to be here when you told us about the baby," Eileen said.

Polly looked at each of the women assembled and then returned her gaze to Eileen. "Debbie said that you were still searching for that baby's mother and that I was one of the women you suspected so long ago."

"That's right," Eileen said. "Do you remember when I called you into my office and questioned you?"

"I do. I was scared out of my wits."

"You didn't look scared. You looked defiant."

"Well, I was scared. I had just run away from my father, and I was afraid you were going to send me back to him. When you started questioning me about the baby, I was relieved." She paused. "But I didn't tell you everything that day."

Debbie leaned forward, clutching her coffee mug.

"I left home because my dad had become overprotective and smothering," Polly said. "He had lost my brother and my mom just a few months apart and was afraid to lose me too. But in his fear of losing me, he kept me almost a prisoner. I was afraid I'd never have any life if I didn't run. So I came here to town and hid out until my twenty-first birthday. That day, I eloped with my boyfriend, Edwin Dorset. We were married for fifty-three years before the Good Lord took him home."

"The baby wasn't yours?" Debbie asked.

"No, ma'am." She looked down at her coffee cup. "The truth is, I couldn't have children. I didn't know it then, but I found out after Edwin and I were married. In the late fifties, I went to see a doctor, and he told me it would be impossible for me. So Edwin and I adopted two children." She smiled, and her whole face lit up with joy. "Two little girls, Amanda and Laura." She chuckled. "They're not so little anymore. Grandmas themselves now."

"Why did you want to come all the way here to tell us this?" Janet asked gently. "Couldn't you have told Debbie over the phone?"

"Well," Polly said, "I came here to tell you what I should have said before, all those years ago. At the time, I was too concerned for my own safety and the plans that Edwin and I had made together. I didn't want to get mixed up in the baby issue any more than necessary."

"What do you mean?" Debbie asked with a frown.

"I saw the woman who left the baby out there." She lifted her hands, as if in defense. "Now, keep in mind that I didn't know what was in the crate until I was questioned and told it was a baby. If I had known she was leaving a baby in the cold, I would have stopped her or grabbed the baby myself. I saw her leave the crate there and then get back on the train."

Debbie leaned forward. "Do you remember what she looked like?"

"My memory isn't as good as it used to be." Polly made a face, and she shook her head. "I don't remember much about it. And I didn't take much notice of her."

"Was she dressed well?" Janet asked.

"Well now, I do remember thinking she was a pretty woman. I had taken to wearing my brother's cast-off clothing because I hadn't learned to sew for myself and I had outgrown my dresses. I remember being jealous of anyone who looked feminine and pretty." She shook her head. "It's been so long ago, I can't recall."

"Was anyone with her?" Eileen asked.

"Not that I remember."

"And you're sure she got back on the train?"

"Yes. I'm positive. I thought it was strange, but I figured she was leaving something for someone else to pick up."

"It had to be Betty," Debbie said. "She and Rebekah were the only single women on the train coming into Dennison, and now we know for certain that whoever left the baby got off and back on the train."

"How will we find Betty?" Janet asked. "No one seems to know where she went."

"I think the answer will be in the letters Katharine is looking for right now." Debbie explained to the others about their trip to Newark and the letters that Clarissa Stewart had exchanged with Betty.

"I hope you're right," Eileen said with a sigh. "I'd sure like to know the answer to this mystery."

Debbie would too.

Several hours later, as Debbie put baked macaroni and cheese into the oven for supper, she heard a knock at her front door. After setting the timer, she wiped her hands on a dish towel and left the kitchen.

As she passed through her living room, she glanced out the window and saw Greg's red truck in her driveway. Nerves fluttered to life in Debbie's midsection as she ran her hand over her head to make sure she didn't have flyaway hair.

She hadn't seen Greg since the dance Friday, and other than a couple of text exchanges about the fundraiser, she hadn't spoken to him either.

Greg smiled as she came around the corner and saw him through the front door window. He lifted a hand, and she smiled back.

"Hi," she said as she opened the door. "Come on in."

"I'm sorry I didn't call first. I have some great news I wanted to share in person."

"It's okay. I don't mind surprise visits. Do you want to come in and sit down?"

"No thanks. I shouldn't stay long. Jaxon has a basketball game tonight, and I need to get home and make supper before he needs to be back at the high school."

Debbie didn't want things to be awkward between her and Greg, but it felt awkward. She couldn't stop thinking about how Marnie had monopolized his time at the dance or how jealous she had felt.

"What's up?" she finally managed to ask.

Greg's smile could light up the room. He looked truly happy. "We sold all the tickets for the dance—two days in advance! There isn't one left. We actually have a wait list started. Everyone is so excited, Debbie."

"We sold out?" Debbie's eyebrows rose at the announcement. "That's wonderful."

"It's all thanks to you. We never sold out for the chili dinner—ever. The dance club from Akron is really looking forward to being here. They plan to do some swing demonstrations. It won't be like the one-on-one lessons we had, but it should help people feel a little more comfortable on the dance floor. And, even better, it should be fun."

"I'm happy for you, Greg. I know this fundraiser means a lot to you."

"I'm happy for all of us—especially the Torrez family. They're the real winners. They'll be at the dance, and they've asked if they can get up and thank everyone for coming. The fundraiser directly benefits their house project, so of course I said yes. They'll also be there Saturday afternoon to help decorate. We're still doing that at three, right?"

Debbie nodded. "I'll pick up the decorations from the Homes for Humanity office tomorrow afternoon and take them over to the depot so they'll be ready for the volunteers on Saturday."

"And you have the meal under control? Do you need help with that?"

"Janet and I will start working on it tomorrow, and then Ian and Tiffany will help her finish on Saturday afternoon while I'm overseeing the decorating." Tiffany, Janet's daughter, was coming home from college for the weekend to pitch in.

"Great." Greg smiled again. "I'll be there at two on Saturday. It'll be a fun day."

"I think so too."

"I should get going, but thanks, Debbie. We couldn't have pulled together this event without you. I want you to know how much I appreciate all you've done."

Debbie didn't feel like she'd contributed a lot—not yet. Saturday would be busy, but she was excited about it.

"Well, thank you for everything you do for the community, Greg. We're all in this together, right?"

He grinned, but then his smile fell. "I'm sorry, again, about the other night. I didn't know Marnie would be at the dance, and—"

"It's okay. Really." Debbie didn't want to talk about it—or think about it.

He nodded. "Bye, Debbie."

"Bye, Greg."

He left and got into his truck.

Debbie stood for a few seconds to watch him pull out of her driveway.

Her phone began to ring in the kitchen, so she jogged back there to answer it before it went to voice mail.

It was Aunt Sherry.

"Hey," Debbie said as she put the phone up to her ear. "How are you?"

"I'm good."

"What can I do for you?"

Aunt Sherry paused and then said, "I've been thinking a lot about the day I was abandoned on the depot platform."

Debbie took a seat at her kitchen table and waited for her aunt to continue.

"You said that Eileen Palmer was the one who found me?"

"No. Harry Franklin found you. Eileen is the one who looked for your birth mother. She took you home and took care of you for several weeks until you were placed with Grandma and Grandpa Albright."

"Eileen took care of me?"

"That's what she said."

"I only know of Eileen from the Dennison Christmas train. I remember riding that with my parents and listening to her share stories about the war years."

Debbie loved the Christmas train, and she loved hearing Eileen's stories. She envied her aunt and anyone else who was fortunate enough to have experienced both at the same time.

"I'd like to tell Eileen who I am," Aunt Sherry said, "and thank her for taking care of me. Do you think she'd like to meet me?"

Debbie grinned. "I think she'd love to meet you. And so would Harry."

"Can you arrange that?"

"I can. When are you free?"

"Maybe tomorrow?"

"I'll see what I can do."

"And don't tell them who I am until we get there, okay? I want to surprise them."

"I think that's a great idea. I'll work out the details and let you know the plan."

"Thanks, Debbie. I appreciate your help. Very much."

"You're welcome. Bye."

"Goodbye, sweetheart."

Debbie immediately dialed Eileen's number. How was she going to keep this a secret from her elderly friend until tomorrow?

And what would Eileen think when she was reunited with Baby Sarah after all these years?

CHAPTER SIXTEEN

"I don't know why I'm so nervous," Aunt Sherry said the next day on their way to Good Shepherd.

Debbie glanced in the rearview mirror and met Janet's gaze. They smiled at each other, and Debbie was thankful that Aunt Sherry had asked them to be part of this reunion. When Aunt Sherry found out that Janet had been helping in the search for her birth mother, she insisted that Janet come along.

"You have every right to be nervous," Debbie said. "You're still getting used to the news. Meeting the woman who took care of you before your mom and dad adopted you is a very big deal."

Aunt Sherry nodded, though she clasped her hands together on her lap and didn't look any more relaxed.

"Have you had a chance to talk to your kids about this?" Debbie asked.

"I'm going to have them over for lunch on Sunday afternoon to share the news. I didn't think it was something I could tell them over the phone."

"I'm sure they'll be supportive," Debbie assured her.

"I hope so. It's hard enough that your dad is still uncomfortable talking to me about it."

Reaching over the console, Debbie placed her hand on Aunt Sherry's. "If you need anyone to talk to, I'm always here for you."

Aunt Sherry unclasped her hands and placed one over the top of Debbie's. "I know, and I'm so thankful for you." She glanced behind her at Janet. "For both of you. Thank you for everything you've done to help me."

Debbie was frustrated that they hadn't found out more about Betty Harper. She was convinced that Betty was Aunt Sherry's birth mother, but it was as if she had disappeared the day she was fired. Debbie had found no trace of her, and if Katharine couldn't find the letters that Betty had written to Katharine's mother, then they had hit another dead end.

Debbie turned in to the parking lot of Good Shepherd, thankful for the warmth of the bright sun shining down on them. The temperatures continued to climb, and the snow had started to melt. The forecast looked promising, with the highest temperature of the week on Saturday—the day of the dance.

After they parked, the three of them got out of the car. Janet was holding a plant that Aunt Sherry brought with them to give to Eileen, and she carried it into the building for her.

"It's not much," Aunt Sherry said, nodding at the small plant. "I wish I could repay her for what she did for me."

"I don't think Eileen would expect to be repaid." Debbie walked beside Aunt Sherry. "She'll be tickled pink to meet you."

Debbie had extended the invitation to Harry as well, but he was out of town at a doctor's appointment and couldn't join them. He planned to be at the dance on Saturday, though, and since Aunt

Sherry was also going to be there, Debbie hoped to introduce them then.

The three of them walked in and were once again greeted by Ashley. After signing in, they headed to the sunroom where Eileen told them she would be waiting.

Aunt Sherry paused outside the room, and Debbie put her hand on her shoulder. "Are you okay?"

Her aunt took a deep breath. "I'm feeling emotional, is all. I'll be fine."

Janet handed the plant to Aunt Sherry, and they walked into the sunroom.

Eileen sat near her monstera plant with her Bible in her lap. She had a blanket over her legs and was dozing in the sunshine. She looked so peaceful, Debbie hated to wake her up, but she knew that Eileen would want to be woken up for this visit.

"Eileen?" Debbie put her hand on Eileen's shoulder.

Eileen blinked her eyes open. "Is it three already?"

Debbie nodded. "It is."

Glancing behind Debbie, Eileen saw Aunt Sherry and Janet. "I didn't know we'd have a whole party." She smiled. "Come on in and have a seat. What a pretty plant you have."

"I brought this for you," Aunt Sherry said as she set it on the table next to Eileen.

"For me?" Eileen frowned. She seemed perplexed as she closed her Bible and set it on the table, next to the plant. "How thoughtful. But I don't have a gift for you."

"You've already given it to me," Aunt Sherry said with tears in her eyes.

Eileen turned her questioning look to Debbie.

"Let's have a seat," Debbie said, "and I'll make the proper introductions."

After they were all seated, Debbie said, "This is my aunt, Sherry Hoffman."

"It's nice to meet you, Sherry," Eileen said.

"And you too." Aunt Sherry wiped at her eyes with a tissue that Janet had handed her.

"We have a surprise for you," Debbie said to Eileen. She turned to Aunt Sherry. "Would you like to tell her?"

Aunt Sherry nodded and wadded up the tissue in her hand. "Mrs. Palmer, I recently found a crate in my garage with some baby items and a newspaper from February fourteenth, 1944."

"Yes, I know about that. Debbie brought it to me." Eileen looked at Aunt Sherry a little closer. "How did you come to possess it?"

"I believe it belonged to me—to my parents. I believe I'm the baby that was found that day."

Eileen's eyes opened wider.

"I had no idea I was adopted until I found the crate in my parents' garage. My birthday—at least the one I've always celebrated—is February fourteenth, 1944—which turns out to be the day the baby was found. After I found the crate, my brother and I had our DNA tested and found out we're not biological siblings. All these discoveries led me to believe that I'm the baby you took care of eighty years ago." She started to cry again, and this time, she let the tears fall. "I wanted to meet you and tell you how thankful I am for everything you did for me. I don't think anyone will know the full extent of your care and sacrifice, except for you. So I want to say thank you. I owe you my life."

Eileen's eyes were still wide as she studied Aunt Sherry. Finally, she reached up and touched Aunt Sherry's cheek, as if she were placing her hand on the face of a baby, and a look of awe filled her gaze. "Sarah?"

Debbie had told Aunt Sherry that Eileen had called her Sarah. Her aunt nodded gently against Eileen's hand.

It was heartwarming to see Eileen looking at Aunt Sherry, at her white hair and deep wrinkles, as if Aunt Sherry were a newborn infant again. "My goodness," Eileen said, tears coming to her eyes. She lowered her hand. "I never thought I'd see you again."

Aunt Sherry laughed and wiped at her cheeks with the tissue. "We've actually met before—just briefly—during a couple of the Christmas train rides."

Eileen shook her head. "To think that I saw you and had no idea who you were. What a wonder this life is sometimes. I didn't know if you had left Dennison or stayed in town. In the forties and fifties, the population of Dennison was twice what it is now. It was easier to get lost in the crowd back then."

Sherry smiled. "I wish I could repay you for your—"

"I'll hear none of that," Eileen said with a chuckle. "I didn't take care of you to get anything in return."

"I know, but I want to offer you something. Debbie said you loved plants, so I brought you this golden pothos. I hope you like it."

Eileen touched one of the leaves. "I love it. Thank you so much. I will think of you every time I look at it." She leaned back in her chair. "So, tell me everything. The last I heard, you had been adopted, but I wasn't given any other information. The adopted parents wanted it that way."

"My parents moved to Dennison right before they adopted me, and I was raised in the house where I now live. They were childless for many years before I came along. I don't know how they came to adopt me, because they never told me I was adopted."

"Maybe they heard about the baby on the platform and approached the social worker from New Philadelphia about you," Debbie suggested. "That might be why they kept it a secret. It would have brought a lot of unwanted attention to you if people had known who you were. And if no one really knew them yet, no one would question a young couple with a brand-new baby."

"Maybe." Aunt Sherry shrugged. "There are a lot of things I won't ever know. But my parents were good parents. They loved me and were kind to me. I have a brother, Vance—Debbie's father. He was born when I was thirteen, so I helped care for him. And I helped care for Debra, who was born four years after Vance and died when she was three. Then I went to business college and became a secretary for a lawyer in New Philadelphia. I ended up falling in love with him." She smiled. "Randy and I had a long and happy marriage. We bought my parents' home after Vance went to college, and raised our two children there. It's been a good life."

Eileen took Aunt Sherry's hand in her own and squeezed it. "I'm so happy to hear that. So very happy."

"I owe it all to you, Mrs. Palmer."

"Call me Eileen—and you don't owe it all to me. Harry Franklin found you. I simply took care of you for a few weeks until your parents took over."

"But if it hadn't been for you—"

"God would have brought someone else along."

"Eileen is a humble woman," Janet said to Aunt Sherry. "She won't take credit even when it's due her."

"Oh." Eileen's eyes shone, and she shook her head. "It was my pleasure. That's all I'll say about that."

"No matter what," Aunt Sherry continued, "you cared for me and sacrificed for me. I take that very seriously. So, thank you."

"You're welcome." Eileen smiled at Sherry. "I'm thankful God put me in the right place at the right time."

Debbie thought of all the places God had put her to offer help to those in need. Most recently, it was her aunt and the Homes for Humanity fundraiser. She still hadn't found all the answers Aunt Sherry was looking for, but she'd keep trying. And she hadn't pulled off the fundraiser dance—not yet—but she was eager to give it all her attention for the next couple of days.

She just hoped everything would go as planned.

"Thank you, again," Aunt Sherry said an hour later as Debbie dropped her off at her house. "I'm looking forward to being at the dance on Saturday. Let me know if you need any help before then."

"You're welcome," Debbie said. "I think we have enough volunteers, but I'll let you know if something comes up."

Aunt Sherry stepped out of the car, and Janet took her place in the front seat. Debbie waited until Aunt Sherry was inside the house and then backed out of her driveway.

"That was fun," Janet said. "I'm glad I was able to go with you."

"I'm happy you could too."

"What a treat for Eileen, especially. She played it down, but I'm sure it was a lot of work to take care of a baby when she wasn't prepared—and working full-time. I remember bringing Tiffany home from the hospital and being completely overwhelmed for weeks—and I was prepared and able to take the time off work to be home with her."

Debbie turned toward downtown Dennison and said, "Do you have any plans this evening?"

"Just getting the house ready for Tiffany's visit. I'm so excited to have her home for the weekend. What about you?"

"I'm going to stop by the Homes for Humanity office after I drop you off, and get the decorations I ordered for the dance. I'll go through them and make sure we have everything we need, and then I'll take them to the depot tomorrow so we have them for Saturday."

"Are there a lot?"

"Quite a bit. Mostly bunting and streamers."

"Do you need some help? I could go to the office with you."

"Okay." Debbie probably didn't need the help, but she would appreciate having Janet there as a buffer between her and Marnie. She hadn't seen Marnie since the dance and wasn't excited about facing her again.

"Then I can meet this infamous Marnie you've told me about," Janet added as if she'd read Debbie's mind.

Debbie drove through town and parked in front of the HOH storefront. She got out, thankful again for the warmer weather, and led Janet toward the building.

"Is Marnie expecting you?"

"Yes. I texted her and told her I would stop by this afternoon."

Debbie opened the office door and found both Marnie and her office assistant, Lexi, at their desks, working. Marnie glanced up, and the congenial look on her face disappeared.

"Ouch," Janet said under her breath. "I feel like the temperature just dropped ten degrees."

"So, it's not my imagination?" Debbie whispered.

"Nope."

They moved into the building and were greeted by Lexi. "Hello."

"Hi," Debbie said. "We're here to get the decorations."

Marnie didn't rise from her desk or greet them.

Lexi looked embarrassed for her as she said, "Hey, Marnie. Do you know anything about decorations?"

"They came last week," Marnie said. "I asked you to move them into the storage room."

"I don't remember moving anything into the storage room," Lexi said, looking confused.

"Those large boxes that were delivered," Marnie said impatiently. "They had red stripes on them."

Lexi shrugged.

Marnie sighed. "Please go and look for them, Lexi. They should be in there."

"We can help," Debbie offered.

Lexi waved for them to follow her and led them through the building to a door in the back. It opened into a large storage room. She flipped on the lights. "I really don't remember moving any boxes in here. I hope we can find them."

"I do too." Debbie hadn't been nervous about the decorations until now. What if they were misplaced—or worse, hadn't been delivered? "The boxes have red stripes?"

"That's what Marnie said." Lexi walked toward the corner while Debbie and Janet spread out into other parts of the room.

"Oh no," Lexi said a couple of minutes later. "It looks like there's been a leak."

"Leak?" Debbie left the pile of boxes she was searching through and joined Lexi in the corner. A large puddle of water was on the floor, with several boxes in the middle of it.

"Has this happened before?" Debbie asked.

"Not that I know of. Maybe it's the melting snow?"

The building was wedged between two other buildings—where would melting snow come from?

Lexi aimed her cell phone light on the boxes. "It looks like these are the decorations."

Sure enough, there were four large boxes with red stripes. The bottom half of each box was soaked.

Debbie's heart sank. Most of the decorations were made of paper. If they didn't have plastic wrapping around them, they would be ruined.

"This is horrible," Debbie said as she reached for one of the boxes. It weighed more than she expected, no doubt from being waterlogged.

"Oh, Debbie," Janet said. "I'm so sorry."

"Let's get them into the front office," Lexi said, "so we can assess the damage."

Debbie looked around but couldn't find the source of the leak. There was nothing coming from the ceiling or from any of the nearby walls. The only water was around her boxes.

A sick feeling hit her in the pit of her stomach. Had someone done this on purpose? Had Marnie? But how would it benefit her to sabotage the fundraiser?

They each carried a box into the front office.

Marnie glanced up and frowned. "Why are those wet?"

"There was a leak in the storage room," Lexi explained as she set her box on the floor. "I'll go back and get the other one."

"A leak?" Marnie rose from her desk. "I didn't know the storage room leaked."

"It hasn't before now," Lexi tossed over her shoulder.

Anger and disappointment welled up inside Debbie, and she had to force herself to not react to the emotion. Accidents happened all the time. But why weren't any of the other boxes ruined?

"Let's get them opened and see what we're dealing with," Janet suggested. She set her box down and opened it.

The streamers were wrapped in plastic bags, and the ones on top looked fine. But as Janet dug down, she groaned. "Most of these are soaked and ruined," she said.

Debbie closed her eyes, so upset she felt like crying. Instead, she opened the box she'd been carrying. It was full of paper bunting, which was also wet.

"It's all ruined," Debbie said. "I can't believe it. What will we do now? This is hundreds of dollars wasted. And we can't order more. It would never get here in time."

"Some of it's okay," Janet said, pointing to the few bags she'd pulled from the top.

"Not nearly enough to fill the lobby."

Janet opened the third box, and it was more of the same. Some of the decorations were okay, but the majority would have to be thrown out.

Marnie didn't say a word—for which Debbie was thankful. She wasn't sure she had the wherewithal to deal with the snarky woman's attitude right now.

Lexi returned with the last box, and it was the same as the others.

"We have about a third of what we need," Janet said, trying to encourage Debbie. "And we have two days before the event. We can make some decorations."

"But we have to prep the meal," Debbie said. "When would we have time?"

"We'll call your aunt Sherry and your mom—and I bet Kim will help. She probably has some patriotic decorations we could borrow. We could even ask Paulette to help." Paulette, Greg's mom, worked as a part-time waitress when they needed extra help in the café. "We can do this!"

Debbie held one of the soaked packages and thought of her options. She needed to focus her energy on fixing this problem, and she couldn't fix it by crying.

She lifted her chin. "Okay. Let's give everyone a call and have them meet at my house in a couple of hours. I'll run to the store and see what supplies I can get. We can order some pizzas for supper and crank out some decorations."

"We can do this," Janet assured her.

It wasn't a foolproof plan, but Debbie wasn't going to let the situation beat her, especially with Marnie standing there, probably waiting for her to fail. She would face this challenge with determination and make it even better than they'd planned.

"I would offer to help," Marnie said with a sigh, "but I'm busy this evening."

"That's okay," Debbie said as she started to separate the salvageable decorations from those that would need to go in the trash. "My friends will step up to help."

"I'll start calling people," Janet said, pulling out her cell phone.

"I said from the beginning that this idea wasn't a good one," Marnie said. "We didn't bother with decorations for the chili dinner, and I can see now that it was for the best."

Debbie stopped sorting the items as Lexi looked on with big eyes.

"You've made your feelings known from the beginning," Debbie said, trying to keep her voice level. "But as much as you want to believe it, this wasn't just my idea. The entire board is excited about this dance. And whether you like it or not, *Greg* is excited about this dance."

"I don't care—"

"This isn't personal, Marnie. We're both trying to help the Torrez family—not impress Greg—and I think that should be our focus. I would appreciate it if you would stop criticizing the fundraiser and start helping make it successful for a family in need."

Marnie's mouth dropped open, and her nostrils flared. She looked like she wanted to say something but snapped her mouth closed, turned on her heel, and stomped back to her desk.

Debbie kept sorting the decorations until she had all the salvageable ones in a new box that Lexi provided. Without saying goodbye to Marnie, Debbie and Janet left the building.

It was going to be a long night, but Debbie was thankful she had support from people who truly cared about her.

CHAPTER SEVENTEEN

*D*ebbie's usually quiet house was full of busy chatter that evening as her friends and relatives worked to make decorations for the fundraiser. Aunt Sherry, Kim, Debbie's mom, and Janet's mom, Lorilee, were there. Debbie called Paulette, and she arrived a few minutes later, eager to be helpful.

"What a shame to lose those decorations," Paulette said as she surveyed the dining room where Mom and Aunt Sherry made streamers out of the red, white, and blue paper that Debbie had found at a discount store in New Philadelphia. Kim and Lorilee were making fabric bunting, and Debbie and Janet were cutting out large stars. "But it looks like these will be even better. What can I do to help?"

"You can jump in where you'd like," Debbie said as she took Paulette's coat.

"I think I'll try my hand at the bunting," Paulette said with a smile.

"Perfect. I'm going to order pizza a little later, so think about what kind you'd like."

"Didn't Greg call you?"

Debbie shook her head. "I haven't heard from him today."

"He and the boys are treating us to supper tonight. They'll be over a little later, if that's okay with you."

"That's great. You must have told him what happened."

"I told him the decorations were ruined by a leak at the office. He said he'd talk to you about it when he stops by later. He has parent-teacher conferences for the boys this evening, or he would have been here by now."

Debbie took Paulette's coat to the entryway closet, wondering what she would tell Greg. She had a hard time believing the "leak" was an accident. It was strange where the water had collected—soaking only her boxes. She didn't like to think what she was thinking, but everything about this situation pointed to Marnie as the guilty party.

She was still mulling it over when she returned to the dining room. It was crowded with everyone working, but it also felt comfortable and cheerful. It reminded Debbie of an old-fashioned quilting bee or something along those lines. She sat back down and resumed her work with Janet.

"I have some interesting news," Aunt Sherry ventured to say during the lull in conversation.

Debbie looked up from the paper star she was cutting out, wondering what Aunt Sherry would say. Was she ready to talk about her adoption? Or was it something else?

"I recently discovered that I was adopted as an infant."

There was a hush in the room. At first, no one seemed to know what to say, and then Lorilee spoke.

"Wow. That's life-changing news, isn't it?"

Paulette asked Aunt Sherry how she came to learn the information. She told them about the crate and the newspaper. Debbie had given her the silver rattle, and she told them about that too.

"Vance and I took a DNA test," Aunt Sherry continued. "It proved we weren't biological siblings, but I still don't know who my birth parents are. Debbie and Janet are working on that."

Debbie glanced at Janet, trying not to let her feelings show. "It hasn't been easy," Debbie conceded. "We've been able to eliminate three women, but there's a fourth, who has eluded us. We can't find anything about her."

"What's her name?" Paulette asked.

"Betty Harper. She was a maid for the Hargreaves family in Newark."

"Wasn't that a really wealthy family?" Lorilee asked. "I remember reading about all the philanthropical work Clarissa Hargreaves Stewart did in the seventies and eighties. She used to donate money to fund projects in small towns all over Ohio. I think she donated a considerable amount of money to our library system over the years."

"She's still alive," Debbie said. "She's in her upper nineties."

"And you said the woman you think might be Sherry's mother worked for the Hargreaves?" Lorilee asked.

"Yes." Debbie told them about Betty having been seen leaving the baby on the depot platform and reboarding the train moments later.

Paulette stopped in the middle of threading her needle. "Was she let go of her position before or after the baby was left in Dennison?" she asked.

"My mom said she was let go the same day," Kim said.

"Maybe Mr. Hargreaves was the baby's father," Mom suggested—and then seemed to remember that they were speaking about Aunt Sherry's potential biological father. She put her hand on Aunt Sherry's arm. "I'm sorry. I shouldn't be so glib."

"It's okay," Aunt Sherry said. "I've already accepted that something horrible happened to my birth mother for her to be so desperate. Or something very scandalous, for her to have left me on the platform."

"And we're certain that you're the baby?" Paulette asked as she pulled the fabric together to make the bunting.

"Not a hundred percent," Aunt Sherry said. "But fairly certain. I won't know for sure unless I can find a blood relative of the birth mother and have our DNA tested to match. My gut, and everything I've learned, tells me that I'm the baby who was abandoned on the platform."

"And you've checked online and all that?" Paulette looked at Debbie. "I'm assuming you've exhausted all options."

Debbie nodded. "We met with Clarissa Stewart and her daughter, Katharine. Clarissa claims that she didn't speak to Betty after she left their employ, but Katharine said that her mother corresponded with Betty for years—or, at least, Betty wrote to her. She's looking for those letters and said she'd contact us if she finds them and if her mother gives her permission to share them with us."

"Why would Betty write to Clarissa Stewart?" Lorilee asked.

"If the baby's father was Mr. Hargreaves," Paulette offered, "perhaps Betty was blackmailing the family."

Several eyebrows rose around the room—including Aunt Sherry's.

"But why drop the baby off in Dennison?" Kim asked. "Why here? Newark is seventy miles away. Did Betty have a connection to Dennison?"

"I never thought of that," Debbie admitted. "I guess I never questioned why here—or where she went after she got back on the train."

"Maybe those questions will be answered when Katharine finds the letters," Janet said.

Debbie frowned. "*If* Katharine finds the letters. Clarissa probably destroyed them if they were full of blackmail. Why would you keep something like that?"

Debbie was placing her final hopes on those letters, but it had been several days and they had heard nothing from Katharine.

"And if she's kept it a secret this long," Janet added, "what makes us think she'll share the information at all?"

Murmurs of agreement filled Debbie's dining room.

"Well," Aunt Sherry said, setting aside another streamer, "I can hope and pray that I get the answers. I've learned a lot already. The truth must be out there somewhere."

Debbie smiled at her aunt. "I'll keep praying with you."

"Me too," the others echoed.

An hour later, as they finished up the decorations, there was a knock at the front door. Debbie left the dining room and found Greg and his boys on her porch, holding several containers in their hands.

"Hey," Debbie said with a welcoming smile. "Come on in."

"Did Mom tell you we'd be here?" Greg asked as Jaxon and Julian entered Debbie's house before him.

"She did. Thank you so much. This is perfect timing. We're just finishing up."

Greg entered with a slow cooker in his hands. "It's nothing fancy. We brought taco fixings."

"Mm. Sounds good to me—and smells good too."

The boys were already getting a warm welcome from the women in the dining room, offering Debbie and Greg a second to themselves.

"Mom told me about the decorations," Greg said with a frown. "Do you know what happened?"

Debbie took a deep breath and shook her head. "All I know for certain is that the only boxes ruined were the decorations, which is a good thing, but I couldn't see where the leak was coming from. It was so strange."

"I've never known that building to leak."

"That's what Lexi said."

"I'm meeting a couple of board members there tomorrow morning to check it out for ourselves. If there's a leak, we need to get it fixed as soon as possible. And if there wasn't a leak..." He let the sentence hang.

Debbie studied him for a heartbeat. "Do you think there's a possibility it wasn't an accident?"

He shrugged. "I have no idea. But Lexi called me this evening and told me she's concerned that it was done on purpose."

Debbie frowned. So she wasn't the only one?

"If you have the time," he said, "could you stop by the HOH office tomorrow morning about nine? I know you're busy at the café, but I'd like to have your perspective on this matter. You saw the boxes and the water. I don't want it to be Lexi's word against Marnie's." He paused and then added quickly, "Unless you're uncomfortable being there."

"It's okay." Debbie said, grateful it was Lexi who had essentially accused Marnie. "I'll try to be helpful."

"Thank you."

Debbie motioned for Greg to follow her. "That looks heavy. Let's go into the kitchen and get everything set up."

They passed through the dining room where everyone was cleaning up their projects. The decorations had turned out better than Debbie had hoped, and there were more than enough to fill the train lobby.

"These look great," Greg said after exchanging greetings. "Thank you all for stepping in to help at the last minute."

"Our pleasure," Lorilee said. "Anything to help Homes for Humanity."

There were nods of agreement all around.

"We'll have supper ready soon," Debbie said. She motioned for Greg and the boys to follow her into the kitchen.

As they prepared supper, Debbie counted her many blessings. At the top of the list were her friends.

Debbie was nervous the next morning when she woke up, and even more nervous as she went about her work at the café. The clock kept ticking closer and closer to nine and the confrontation they might have with Marnie.

Janet knew about the upcoming meeting at the Homes for Humanity building and had asked Paulette if she could come in and help while Debbie was gone. Debbie hoped it wouldn't be for more than thirty minutes or so. Thankfully, the building was less than a block away and the morning rush was slowing down.

"I'm going to head over to the meeting," Debbie said to Janet about five minutes to nine.

Paulette was taking care of the customers in the dining room, and Janet was busy putting away the load of dishes she had just washed.

"How are you feeling?" Janet asked, wiping her hands on a dish towel.

"Sick to my stomach. If Marnie isn't guilty, it's not going to sit well with her to be accused. And if she is guilty, I have no idea what kind of consequences she'll face."

"I'm sure Greg and the other board members will deal with whatever happens. He just wants your testimony, right?"

"I think that's all."

"You have my full support," Janet said. "I was there, and I thought things looked strange too. If he needs to talk to me, have him give me a call or stop by here. I'm happy to tell him what I saw."

"Thanks." Debbie took a deep breath, hating the nervous flutter in her stomach. "I'll be back as soon as I can."

"There's no hurry. It'll probably be quiet in here for the next hour or so, and Paulette and I can handle it."

"Call me if we get a rush."

"Will do." Janet gave her an encouraging smile.

Debbie grabbed her coat and slipped it on before she left the café.

It was warm again today, and the snow in the street was turning to muddy slush. Debbie stepped over several puddles on her way down the sidewalk and across the road.

Greg's red truck was parked outside the Homes for Humanity office, so Debbie felt comfortable walking inside the building.

Two board members stood with Greg and Marnie. Marnie looked perplexed and confused, but when she saw Debbie, the confusion turned to anger.

"Does this have something to do with the ridiculous decorations?" Marnie asked. "Is that why you're all here? Because Debbie complained?"

Greg took a deep breath and smiled at Debbie. "Thanks for coming," he said.

Debbie just nodded, not wanting to make the situation worse by saying something that might stir up Marnie.

"Well?" Marnie had crossed her arms and was tapping her foot. "Can you tell me now why you've all come?"

Lexi was seated at her desk, watching with a wary expression. "*I* called Greg," she said. She stood up and joined the group. "Not Debbie."

Marnie turned her frown on her assistant. "But what did you call him about?"

"Before we go any further," Greg said, putting a pause in their conversation, "I want to say that this is just an investigation. No one is making accusations or pointing fingers. I was informed, yesterday, by Lexi, that there was an accident in the storage room and that several hundred dollars' worth of damage was done. I called Matt and Kayla to come and look at the storage room so we can figure out what happened. As a nonprofit organization that answers to a lot of people, we need to be good stewards of our finances. We can't let this happen again, if we can prevent it."

"Then why is she here?" Marnie asked, tilting her head toward Debbie.

"Debbie is on the subcommittee for the fundraiser. Not only that, she was here yesterday and saw what happened. I want as many testimonies as possible so we can make an accurate report of this incident." He looked at Lexi. "Can you show us where you found the boxes and the leak?"

Lexi nodded and led the way out of the room.

As the others passed, Greg waited for Debbie to join him. "I'm happy you're here," he said. "I know this isn't easy."

Debbie tried to smile, but it felt half-hearted.

They entered the storage room behind the others. Lexi had already shown the other board members where the puddle was located. There were wet towels on the floor, as if someone had tried to deal with the problem but hadn't quite succeeded.

"Who put these towels here?" Greg asked.

"I did." Marnie lifted her chin. "I didn't want the puddle to ruin anything else."

"Where is the leak coming in?" Kayla asked.

Marnie shrugged. "I don't know. I'm not a contractor."

"I am," Greg said, though everyone knew it. "I'll see what I can find."

As he and Matt looked around the storage room, Marnie, Lexi, Kayla, and Debbie stood quietly and watched. Debbie didn't hazard a glance at Marnie, since she knew she'd be met with an icy glare.

After a few minutes, Greg and Matt came back to the puddle. Greg let out a deep sigh. "I couldn't find any leaks. Did you see anything, Matt?"

Matt shook his head, his face grim.

"What I did find," Greg said, "was a garden hose hooked up to the water spigot in the furnace room." He turned to Marnie and Lexi. "Do either one of you know why?"

Lexi shook her head.

Marnie frowned but didn't say anything.

Greg shared a look with the other board members. "How much damage was done to the decorations?" he asked Debbie.

"At least two-thirds of them were ruined."

"Can you estimate the cost?"

Debbie gave him the cost of the ruined items, as well as the additional cost of supplies to make replacement decorations.

He returned his gaze to Kayla and Matt. "Do you think it's safe to say this was an intentional act? And not an accident?"

"I think it's safe to say that," said Kayla, and Matt nodded his agreement.

"That leads us to question those who had access to this building," Greg continued as he looked from Marnie to Lexi and back again. "Can either of you explain this?"

Lexi looked bewildered, and she shook her head.

Marnie bit her lip and then said, "It was me."

"Why?" Greg didn't seem surprised at her admission.

Marnie shrugged. Her disdain was evident on her face. "This entire event has been a debacle from the beginning."

"A debacle?" Debbie asked. "What do you mean?"

"It has cost more money to put on than any of our other events, and I wanted our board to see that the extra expense was frivolous and ridiculous."

"By wasting money?" Greg asked.

"Why not? It was all wasted anyway. Decorations are unnecessary, and if I couldn't get the rest of you to realize that by using common sense, I had to think of another way."

"This event is raising more money than the chili dinners did," Kayla said. "So a little extra investment up front was well worth the effort."

Marnie crossed her arms and pursed her lips, as if she was done with the conversation.

"Unfortunately," Greg said after a moment's pause, "I think we're going to have to ask you to leave, Marnie."

Her eyes opened wide. "Are you serious?"

"This is unacceptable behavior," he said. "Unbecoming of our executive director. You're on suspension until the board can meet to discuss the status of your employment."

"You've got to be kidding." She stared at him. "All because of a little water damage?"

"Please pack your things and go." Greg remained stoic. "We'll ask Lexi to fill in for you until we meet next week. Consider yourself on administrative leave until we can determine our next course of action."

Marnie looked ill, as if she couldn't believe what he was saying. She shook her head, turned around, and came face-to-face with Debbie.

"This is all your fault," she sputtered. "If you hadn't—"

"That's enough," Greg said. "Please leave, Marnie."

She pressed her lips together and lifted her chin before brushing past Debbie.

Kayla and Matt followed her into the office, and Lexi joined them, leaving Debbie and Greg alone in the storage room.

"I'm sorry about that," Greg said, looking troubled.

"It's not your fault."

"No, but I represent the organization, and I'm embarrassed about what happened."

"You don't need to be."

He smiled at Debbie. "Thank you. You've been kinder than we deserve."

Debbie returned his smile.

It didn't take long for Marnie to storm out of the office.

Debbie wasn't sad to see her leave. Now they could turn their time and attention to things that mattered, like raising money for the Torrez family.

CHAPTER EIGHTEEN

*a*n hour later, Debbie was cleaning a table after two customers left the café. When she'd returned, she'd filled Janet in on what had taken place with Marnie. Now the café was quiet, and it gave her time to think about what had just happened at the HOH office. She hated to see Marnie lose her job, but it was obvious that the woman wasn't the right person for the position. It was a sad situation, but in the long run, she knew it was probably best for the organization if Marnie left.

"Feeling better?" Janet asked when she came into the dining room.

"Some. But I still feel horrible about what happened."

Janet opened the bakery case and took inventory of the items inside. "It's never easy to confront someone. It sounds like Greg handled the situation well."

Debbie nodded. "I'm ready to move on and focus on the fundraiser."

"Me too." Janet pulled out a couple of trays. "It looks like the apple-cinnamon muffins are popular. I'll have to rotate them into the menu more often."

The café door opened, and Katharine Crawford walked in. She wore a long wool coat and black leather gloves. An oversized designer shoulder bag was slung over her arm.

"Hello," Debbie said, almost too surprised to speak. She hadn't expected Katharine to come all the way to Dennison—especially unannounced.

"I hope it's okay that I stopped by without calling first," Katharine said, looking a little uncomfortable.

"Of course it is." Debbie put the rag and disinfectant spray she had been using under the counter. "Come in. We're happy to see you."

"Would you like something to eat or drink?" Janet asked.

"Oh." Katharine glanced at the menu board and then at the bakery case. "I suppose a cup of coffee and a blueberry muffin would be nice."

Debbie got the coffee while Janet plated a muffin. Katharine took a seat at the counter, took off her gloves, and laid them aside.

"I suppose you're surprised to see me," she said.

"Surprised and pleased," Debbie assured her. "We're so happy you came all this way. I hope it means that you found something helpful."

Katharine pressed her lips together and nodded, looking neither pleased nor upset. "I did find something. Something that was very shocking, actually."

Debbie remembered the women making conjectures about Betty Harper and Mr. Hargreaves and wondered if they had been close to the truth.

"How about we take a break and join you?" Janet asked. "We can talk about what you've discovered."

"Okay." Katharine grabbed her things and moved from the counter to a table nearby. She set her bag on the floor and arranged the blueberry muffin and coffee cup in front of her.

Debbie shared a look with Janet and then filled two more cups with coffee. She carried them to the table and took a seat while Janet brought over a couple of muffins for them.

Katharine got right to the point. "I'm not going to lie. The past few days have been very difficult for me. I had no idea the secrets my mother was keeping until you two arrived and piqued my interest. I went into the attic to look for the letters my mother had received from Betty and learned more than I ever anticipated. It has taken me a couple of days to digest the information."

Debbie waited for her to continue.

"I found Betty's letters," Katharine said. "She wrote every year around the time of the baby's birthday, demanding money from my mother to keep her quiet. She did this until her death—or so I assume—in 1987. The last letter Betty wrote said she was ill, and then there were no more."

"She was blackmailing your mother?" Janet asked.

"Yes." Katharine nodded. "For over forty years. And she made a substantial income from it too. Plenty enough to live on."

It was Debbie's turn to ask a question. "Do you know why?"

"I'm afraid I do." Katharine reached down, opened her bag, and pulled out a bundle of envelopes. "There are forty-three letters in all. The first one, dated February fourteenth, 1945, told me everything I needed to know about what had happened. The rest of them were short and simple, reminding my mother of her obligation."

"And your mother paid her the money every year?"

Katharine shrugged. "I believe so. Betty always received the same amount, according to my grandfather's financial logs. It didn't say the money was going to Betty, but it was the same amount each year, and on the memo line it simply said 'personal expense.'" She took the first letter off the top of the stack and held it out to Debbie. "Everything you'll want to know is in this one."

Debbie didn't reach out and take the letter. Instead, she studied Katharine. "So your mother gave you permission to share these with us?"

Katharine nodded. "I had many long conversations with my mother. She finally agreed to let me bring these letters to you. I told her that her secret is eighty years old and it's time to set the record straight. Her actions affected the lives of many people. I no longer care about her pride or her reputation. This needs to be brought out into the open for healing."

Debbie took the letter, wondering what information it might hold to answer the questions that had been troubling her for weeks.

"After you read the letter," Katharine said, "I have a few more things I want to tell you—and also something I need to ask you."

Debbie gently removed the letter from the yellowed envelope. Her heart pounded fast as she unfolded the paper and laid it flat on the table.

Betty's handwriting wasn't elegant or formal. It was almost hard to read with the tall, skinny loops and the faded ink. Debbie had to get close to make out the words.

But when she did, everything became clear.

February 14, 1945

A year has passed since I left Newark, and I've thought of writing this letter to you every day since then. You're probably surprised to hear from me. You probably hoped that you would never have to think about me again. But I've thought a lot about you and that final day working in the house. I've changed a lot since then. I'm no longer the quiet, shy girl I used to be. I know how to get what I want now.

I used the money you gave me, and I got as far away as I could. I know you said you never wanted to hear about the baby again, but I have a good reason for writing this letter. Just remember, none of this was my fault. I happened to be in the wrong place at the wrong time.

You've probably guessed by now that I'm not going to keep this secret if I'm not compensated in some way. I know that if the truth got out, your family's stellar reputation in the community would be ruined. Your father's business would suffer, your prospects for a good marriage would disappear, and your mother would be devastated. You're lucky she was in Europe when it all happened. She can still learn the truth with a simple note or a phone call from me. I know you don't want that to happen. My question is, what's it worth to you to make sure it doesn't?

What about the baby's father? What is it worth to keep this secret from him? His family is even more important than yours. You didn't think I knew who you were seeing, but I did. I know he's a senator—and that he has a wife and children. How would they feel? And what would the newspapers do with a scandalous story that would ruin his hopes for another term in Washington? Does he even know he has another child? If you choose not to pay me, I can always go to him.

I've been wondering how you kept your pregnancy a secret from your father and the rest of the staff for so long.

I didn't suspect anything until that last day. You were so clever in hiding it. If I hadn't come across you delivering the baby by yourself in the bathroom, how could you have kept it hidden? The money you gave me to get away with her was nice—for a time—but the baby and I cannot live off it forever. I've come to New York City, and it's expensive to live here, especially since I can't get a job, what with the baby and all.

Yes, that's right. I kept the baby. I told you I knew a nice family who would take her in, but then I got to thinking how much better it would be for me to keep her. For insurance purposes, so to speak.

I know you have moved on with your life. Your mother and father probably have no idea that their precious daughter got herself in trouble with a married man, or that you've covered up a great scandal by paying a maid to keep her mouth shut.

There are only two of us who know the truth. I'm the only one who has nothing to lose—and maybe something to gain—by sharing it with the world. I expect a check in the mail within the next week, and if it is not as generous as I believe it should be, I will not hesitate to sound the alarm.

And, just to make sure that you can't say that it's a maid's word against your own, I took the silver rattle, the one given to your family by President Ulysses S. Grant. It has your great-grandfather Benjamin Hargreaves' initials engraved in the silver. If you deny this story, I will simply produce the baby and share the details of the rattle, since your father

*often told people about it and his family's connection to the
famous general and president.*

*Do not hesitate to respond to me, Clarissa. I have the
power to make your life miserable. And I will.*

Betty Harper

Debbie looked up from reading the letter, stunned. She handed
it to Janet. Debbie remained silent as she waited for Janet to finish.
When she did, she glanced up, her surprise just as evident as the
shock Debbie felt.

"Wow," Debbie finally said as she handed the letter back to
Katharine. "So your mother really is my aunt's birth mother?"

Katharine folded the letter and put it back in the envelope.
"When I confronted her with these letters, she denied everything, as
I suspected she would. But I have all of them, as well as my grandfather's financial logs, which he was diligent to keep, and it showed a
significant sum of money paid every February. With all this evidence, she couldn't deny it for long. She eventually told me the whole
story. She fell in love with a married senator. She'd met him through
her father's connections while she was away at boarding school.
After she graduated and came home for the summer, she discovered
she was pregnant. Her mother had been in Europe for some time,
and her father was absent with his work. She somehow hid the pregnancy from the staff and stayed home for most of that year."

Debbie held her cup of coffee but was too transfixed to even
sip it.

"The day she gave birth, the maid, Betty Harper, found her in
the bathroom and helped her with the delivery. Mother didn't know

what to do. She was frantic. And then, as the letter says, Betty offered to take the baby to people she knew who would love her as their own. Mother paid Betty a handsome fee to take the baby away early the next day. A year later, when she received this letter, she was almost prostrate with grief, knowing that her daughter was being raised by a woman with such a depraved character. There was no way she could pay Betty enough to keep her quiet. She had to tell her father what had happened. Mother never saw her again but received these letters from her every year as a reminder."

"And she never told her mother?" Janet asked.

Katharine shook her head.

"But Betty left the baby in Dennison!" Debbie exclaimed. "She didn't raise her!"

"No, she didn't," Katharine said. "My mother was deceived by Betty Harper at every turn. Every year, Betty related how she was raising the child, listing the many expenses she incurred, and demanding payment. The day you came to see us was the first Mother knew that Betty's deception and guile went much further than she could have ever guessed." Her eyes softened. "But even with all the guilt and sadness she's felt in the last few days, there is one blessing that my mother has clung to. Her baby was brought up in a loving home after all."

"She needed your mother to believe that she still had the baby," Debbie said.

"Yes," Katharine said. "It was essential that my mother believe that Betty had at her fingertips the power to ruin her. And now Mother is dealing with the awful truth that her baby was abandoned on a railway platform."

She let out a breath. "Now, I believe this quest to find answers started because your aunt discovered the crate and the rattle that came with the baby."

"That's right," Debbie said. "And then she discovered that she and my father do not have the same DNA—and because she is older than he is and remembers when their mother was pregnant with him, she is the adopted one."

"Then I believe that your aunt is my half sister," Katharine said. "And I would like to introduce her to my mother—our mother—if she would like. My mother has agreed to a meeting, if it is kept quiet between us. She is an old woman now, and she does not want to disrupt anyone's life more than she already has."

"I completely understand," Debbie said. "I will speak to my aunt Sherry and see what she thinks."

"If she agrees," Katharine said, "I would like to have the meeting soon. Today or tomorrow, if possible."

"As far as I know, that would be fine," Debbie said.

"Thank you," Katharine said. "I will wait to hear from you."

"I appreciate all that you've done. It will mean everything to Aunt Sherry to have answers."

It meant a lot to Debbie too. She couldn't believe they had finally unraveled this mystery.

Even if the answer was jarring.

CHAPTER NINETEEN

There was no time to waste. Debbie and Janet closed the café a few minutes early to drive to Aunt Sherry's house. They needed to start preparing the food for the fundraiser, but that would have to wait. If they wanted to get to Newark and back before nightfall, they needed to leave as soon as possible.

"Will she even be home?" Janet asked as they drove toward Aunt Sherry's house.

"I hope so. I should have called, but all I could think about was telling her in person."

"It's a huge deal," Janet agreed. "Who would have ever thought that your aunt Sherry would be Clarissa Stewart's biological daughter?"

"My grandparents were amazing," Debbie said. "But they lived a very humble life. To know that Aunt Sherry is the daughter of Clarissa Hargreaves and an influential senator is pretty shocking information."

"I wonder if your grandparents ever suspected?"

"I highly doubt it. No one seemed to know where the baby came from, as we've learned, and I don't think they ever had a clue."

"Do you think she'll want to meet Clarissa?"

Debbie shrugged. "I don't know. This is all still so new to everyone."

"I wonder what Clarissa is thinking. To know that your child is out there, never expecting to meet her, and then you find out who she is eighty years later? That's pretty mind-boggling stuff to deal with."

"I can't even imagine."

Debbie pulled into the driveway, and they got out of the car.

Before they were at the door, Aunt Sherry opened it, smiling. "This is a nice surprise. Come on in. I'm just sorting and packing. It's all I ever do anymore."

Debbie and Janet walked across Aunt Sherry's front porch and then into her foyer. The house was warm, and a television was on in the living room.

"What brings you out my way?" Aunt Sherry asked as she looked from Debbie to Janet. "I hope it isn't bad news."

"It's not," Debbie said. "It's not bad news, but it's serious."

Aunt Sherry frowned and motioned for them to step into her living room. She turned off the TV and indicated they should have a seat.

"What's going on?" she asked Debbie.

Debbie took a deep breath. "We've learned who your birth mother is."

Aunt Sherry stared at Debbie for a long time, her emotions unreadable.

"Clarissa Hargreaves's daughter came by the café today," Debbie said. "You remember, she told us that Betty Harper wrote to Clarissa—"

"Yes," Aunt Sherry said, a bit impatient. "I remember. Was Betty my mother?"

Debbie shook her head. "Katharine brought the letters to us. She received one each year in February, demanding money so Betty would keep quiet."

"Betty was blackmailing Clarissa?" Aunt Sherry studied Debbie, as if trying to put all the pieces of the puzzle together.

"Yes. Clarissa was the one who was pregnant. Betty found Clarissa having a baby—the baby that was left on the platform—"

"Me."

Debbie nodded. "She hid the pregnancy from everyone, but Betty discovered the truth. Apparently, Clarissa had an affair with a married senator while she was away at school the year before."

Aunt Sherry's mouth fell open, and she blinked several times, but she didn't speak.

"Clarissa paid Betty to take the baby to a family Betty told her about. But Betty lied to her. We know that she dropped the baby off at the depot, and can only hope that she did so because she knew there were women working at the canteen who could take care of her—of you."

"And every year, around the time of my birthday, Betty wrote to Clarissa, demanding more money to keep the secret to herself."

"Yes," Debbie said. She hoped what she had to say next wouldn't upset her aunt too much. "But in her letters, Betty told Clarissa that she'd kept the baby and was raising it on her own. Every year she asked for money to help pay for expenses and reminded her that failure to pay would result in Clarissa's world crashing down around her."

Aunt Sherry rubbed her forehead as she looked down at the box of clothing she had been sorting.

No one spoke for a few seconds. Debbie wanted to give Aunt Sherry some time to process the information she'd just heard.

"How did Clarissa meet the senator?" Aunt Sherry finally asked.

Debbie explained that Clarissa knew the senator through her father.

"He was married with a family," Debbie said. "We don't know anything else about him."

"Did he know about me?"

"We don't have any reason to believe that he did."

Aunt Sherry stood. "This is a lot to digest."

"There's more," Janet said. "Clarissa would like to meet you, if you're willing."

"Meet me?" Aunt Sherry asked, incredulous.

"Today, if possible."

"Today?" Aunt Sherry's eyes opened wide.

"I know it's soon," Debbie acknowledged. "But Katharine asked if it could be today or tomorrow, and tomorrow—"

"You're busy with the fundraiser." Aunt Sherry took a deep breath. "I suppose it doesn't matter when it happens. Whether it's today or next year, it'll be awkward."

"Are you available to go now?" Debbie asked. "It's a little over an hour's drive."

"Well, let me see." Aunt Sherry looked around the room. "I'll need to put on something more presentable. Can you wait a few minutes?"

"Of course. Take all the time you need. We'll be here."

Aunt Sherry nodded. "I'll try to be quick."

After she left the room, Debbie turned to Janet. "I can't imagine what she's feeling right now."

"She's fortunate to have you. At least she doesn't have to do this alone."

"No, but it must still feel lonely."

They waited for about twenty minutes as Aunt Sherry changed and got ready to leave. When she reappeared in the living room, she held the silver rattle in her hands.

"I've been curious about this," Aunt Sherry said. "It must be valuable. Do you think she'll want it back?"

"I'm not sure, but you're right. It's actually very valuable," Debbie told her. "In one of her letters, Betty said Ulysses S. Grant gave it to Clarissa's great-grandfather. It has his initials, BH, for Benjamin Hargreaves."

Aunt Sherry looked down at the rattle, her eyes huge. "What?"

"I'm sure there's more to the story," Debbie said. "Perhaps Clarissa will tell you."

"I don't want to keep it, if it's that valuable."

"You can give it back to her if you'd like." Debbie stood from the couch and joined her aunt. "She might like to have it again. It sounds like it meant a lot to her father."

"I can see why." Aunt Sherry gently placed the rattle in her purse.

"Are you ready?" Debbie asked.

"I think so. How does my hair look?"

Smiling, Debbie put her hand on her aunt's back to lead her to the front door. "You look beautiful, as always."

Aunt Sherry stopped and studied Debbie, her face serious. "Do you think she'll be disappointed in me? I'm not fancy or refined. Will she be embarrassed by me?"

Debbie shook her head. "Of course not! Aunt Sherry, you are a lovely woman, and you have nothing to be ashamed of. You know your worth has nothing to do with wealth or possessions. It has everything to do with being a child of God. You don't need to own anything fancy to be priceless. You're worth far more than rubies or diamonds, simply because you were created in the image of God. Nothing else matters."

Aunt Sherry put her hand on Debbie's cheek, unshed tears in her eyes. "Thank you, sweetheart. That's the reminder I needed."

Debbie hugged her aunt and then led her outside. Janet sat in the back of the car while Aunt Sherry got into the passenger's seat. She placed her purse on her lap and lifted her chin. "I'm praying that God gives me the strength and courage to do this."

"If it's any consolation," Janet said, "I have a feeling that Clarissa and Katharine are probably just as nervous as you are, or maybe even more so."

"I'll send Katharine a text and tell her we're coming," Debbie said before she pulled out of the driveway. "She's probably back in Newark by now."

Debbie sent a quick text and almost immediately got one in return.

"They'll be waiting for us," she said. "Are you ready?"

With a decisive nod, Aunt Sherry said, "Let's go before I chicken out."

Debbie smiled, but she was still apprehensive.

What if Clarissa was cold and unwelcoming? Debbie would hate to see Aunt Sherry hurt even more.

The drive to Newark felt much longer this time. Maybe it was because Debbie knew what waited for them at the other end of the journey. Or maybe it was the nerves she felt for Aunt Sherry.

Her aunt talked a mile a minute the entire way. It was obvious she was anxious, and her anxiety came out in words. She told story after story about her childhood, almost as if she was reminding herself that she'd had a good one.

"I was raised as an only child until I was thirteen," she told Janet. "Until Vance came along. He was a cutie, to be sure, but he was so annoying."

Debbie chuckled.

"I'm being serious," Aunt Sherry said. "He cried all the time, and then he was always climbing on something or trying to get out of the house. I always felt like we had accomplished a huge feat if he was still alive at the end of the day."

She continued telling them about some of her earliest memories. Camping trips they had taken. Family reunions they had attended.

Finally, they passed the Newark city limits, and Aunt Sherry grew quiet.

"I've never been here before," she said after a few minutes. "It's a pretty town."

"The Hargreaves were some of the wealthiest people in Newark," Debbie said. "They owned the glassmaking factory and lived in one of the nicest houses in town."

Aunt Sherry nodded. "I've heard the name before but don't know much about them. Who would have guessed that I'd be connected to their family? Do you think I look like them?"

Debbie hadn't thought much about it, but now that Aunt Sherry mentioned it, she did see a resemblance between her and Katharine. Their eyes had the same shape, and so did Clarissa's.

"I think so."

When Debbie finally pulled into the driveway on the Diamond Willow property, Aunt Sherry leaned forward and stared at the house.

"*This* is Clarissa's home?"

"Impressive, isn't it?" Debbie asked. She told Aunt Sherry how the Hargreaves had built the house and then turned it into a retirement home when Clarissa could no longer keep up the maintenance on the property.

"So this is where I was born." Aunt Sherry shook her head. "I never thought to ask my mom anything about my birth. I wonder what she would have said. Would she have told me the truth? I doubt it. Back then people didn't talk about adoption like they do now."

Debbie patted Aunt Sherry's knee and then parked the car.

When she turned off the engine, the three of them sat there for a minute, staring at the massive house.

"Are you ready to do this?" Debbie asked her aunt.

"No, but I don't think I'll ever be ready." Aunt Sherry grabbed the door handle and took a deep breath. "Let's go."

They got out of the car and walked into the house.

After climbing the steps from the entry, they were greeted by a different receptionist.

"Hello," she said. "May I help you?"

"Mrs. Stewart is expecting us," Debbie said.

"Do you know how to get to her apartment?"

"Yes." Debbie looked at her aunt. "Can you climb the stairs, or would you like to use the elevator?"

"There's an elevator?" Aunt Sherry whispered.

Debbie smiled. "You don't need to whisper, but yes."

"That would be fun."

The receptionist motioned for them to follow her.

They walked through another hallway and into a beautiful foyer. The woodwork was dark and polished to a gleam. Ornate wallpaper covered the walls, and thick rugs graced the wood floors. Debbie peeked into a front parlor and a formal dining room. The ceilings were impossibly high, and the furniture was elegant and beautiful.

An elderly woman sat in one of the parlors with a book in hand and a small white dog on her lap. She glanced up at them with a curious smile. The receptionist nodded a greeting, but they continued on without stopping to say hello.

Aunt Sherry looked around with her mouth slightly ajar, her purse hanging over her forearm.

"The elevator is over here," the receptionist said. "Mrs. Stewart is on the second floor."

"Thank you." Debbie entered the small elevator, followed by Aunt Sherry and Janet, who pressed the button for the second floor. There was a button for a third floor and for the basement as well.

After a short ride, the elevator stopped, and the door opened. They were right across the hallway from Clarissa's apartment.

Family pictures adorned the walls. Photos from several generations. Some austere and foreboding, others warm and gentle.

A woman in a white nurse's uniform stepped out of a room down the hallway but didn't seem to notice them as she walked in the opposite direction.

"Ready?" Debbie asked Aunt Sherry again.

She nodded. "I think so."

Debbie crossed the hallway and knocked on the door.

After a moment Katharine opened the door, nodded at Debbie, and then stared at Aunt Sherry.

Debbie wasn't sure how she had missed the similarities between them before. They were almost the exact same height, had the same eyes, and the same nose.

"Sherry?" Katharine asked.

Aunt Sherry nodded and managed a smile.

"Thank you for coming," Katharine said. "I'm Clarissa's daughter, Katharine Stewart Crawford."

Aunt Sherry extended her hand. "I'm Sherry Hoffman. Hoffman is my married name. My maiden name is Albright."

"It's a pleasure to meet you." Katharine shook her hand, a warm smile on her face. "Have you been told about the letters?"

"Yes. My niece, Debbie, has told me everything."

Relief crossed Katharine's face. "Good." She looked at Debbie. "Thank you."

"Of course."

"Won't you come in?" Katharine moved to the side. "Mother is anxious to meet you."

"Is she well?" Aunt Sherry asked.

"She gets along," Katharine said. "Though she's frail, she hides it well."

They entered the apartment, and Debbie was impressed with the opulence all over again. She couldn't imagine being raised in such luxury.

Clarissa was in her sitting room today, waiting.

When they entered, Debbie saw Clarissa's and Aunt Sherry's gazes collide.

A hush fell over the room as neither one moved or spoke.

Finally, Katharine moved farther into the room and said, "Mother, you remember Debbie Albright and Janet Shaw. And this is Sherry Albright Hoffman."

Clarissa slowly rose from her chair and walked across the room, her eyes on Sherry.

The resemblance between them was remarkable. The eyes, nose, and even the way they held their shoulders was similar.

"I would have called you Penelope," Clarissa said in a quiet, gentle voice. "But you are a beautiful Sherry."

"I've only just learned about my past," Aunt Sherry managed through her tears. "I didn't know until earlier this month that I was adopted. This is all very new to me."

"I've known for eighty years, and it feels new to me too." Clarissa extended her hands.

Sherry placed hers inside them.

They stood for a few more moments, studying each other. They were both old women with white hair, deep wrinkles, and much life experience, less than two decades apart in age. But, for this moment, they were mother and child again.

Debbie, Janet, and Katharine looked on, but it was as if they weren't even in the room.

A tear fell down Clarissa's cheek. Finally, she said, "I'm sorry, Sherry. I truly had no idea that you were abandoned on that platform. Will you forgive me?"

Without hesitation, Aunt Sherry nodded. "Yes, of course."

A smile lit Clarissa's face, making her look decades younger. She pulled Aunt Sherry into her embrace and closed her eyes. "Thank you."

Tears streamed down Katharine's cheeks, and Debbie had to find a tissue for herself.

When Clarissa finally drew back, she took Aunt Sherry's hand again and led her over to the sofa.

Debbie, Janet, and Katharine followed them. There was a tea set on the coffee table. It was just as beautiful and elegant as the rest of the house.

Katharine began to pour tea for everyone as Clarissa turned toward Aunt Sherry.

"There is so much to say," Clarissa said. "A lifetime to catch up on. I'm sure you have questions."

Aunt Sherry took her purse off her arm and set it on the floor next to her. "First, I have something for you."

Clarissa watched as Debbie's aunt pulled the silver rattle from her purse. It was shiny and bright and looked almost brand-new since Debbie had polished it.

Clarissa's eyes lit up, and her lips parted. She tenderly took the rattle from Aunt Sherry's hands, shaking her head. "I never thought I'd see this again."

"I've heard there's a special story to this rattle," Aunt Sherry said.

"Yes." Clarissa ran her gnarled fingers over the shiny surface. "My great-great-grandfather, Thomas Hargreaves, was a lieutenant colonel in the Union Army and served alongside Ulysses S. Grant during the Civil War. They were good friends. General Grant stood as his best man at his wedding. When my great-grandfather, Benjamin Hargreaves was born in 1863, Ulysses gave Thomas this rattle for the baby." She pointed to the initials. "It was accompanied by a note, which I still have. This rattle was passed down from generation to generation and sat in a place of prominence in my father's study."

Clarissa reached out and took Aunt Sherry's hand and gently placed the rattle in her palm. When she looked up, she met Aunt Sherry's gaze and smiled. "It is yours and should be passed down to your children and your grandchildren, and their children after them. Before you leave, I'll get the note for you as well."

Aunt Sherry shook her head. "I couldn't possibly—"

"I insist." Clarissa closed Aunt Sherry's fingers around the rattle. "You should have had so much more, Sherry. In my immaturity and foolishness, I stole your birthright from you. It's something I've regretted my entire life. I don't deserve the blessing God has given me by bringing you back into my life, but I will accept it with open arms. I hope this will not be the last time I see you. Do you have children?"

Aunt Sherry nodded. "A son and a daughter—and grandchildren and great-grandchildren too."

"I would like to meet all of them, if you'll let me," Clarissa said. "I'd like them to meet my children and grandchildren as well. And…" She paused and looked at Katharine, who nodded. "I would like to change my will. I didn't give you the life you deserved, but it isn't too late to ensure that you and your family are blessed by our family's good fortune."

Aunt Sherry shook her head, but Clarissa put up her hand. "I won't hear your protests."

"I don't even know for sure that I'm your biological daughter," Aunt Sherry said.

"If it makes you feel better," Clarissa said, "I will gladly give a sample for a DNA test. But I only have to look at you to know you're my daughter, Sherry. I have no doubt in my mind."

Debbie didn't either.

"I do have one question," Aunt Sherry said, tentatively.

"You may ask me anything."

"Did my father know?"

Clarissa looked at her hands, which were clasped in her lap. She shook her head, heaviness weighing down her countenance. "No. I never expected to see him again. It was a foolish relationship that was doomed to failure from the beginning. We both knew it and didn't care. I left Massachusetts and came home to Ohio, not realizing I was pregnant. I tried to ignore the signs for a very long time. Perhaps it was denial. I'm not sure. But when I knew for certain, I was several months along and knew I couldn't tell anyone—least of all the father." She looked up at Aunt Sherry. "I'm so sorry. He is long gone, and his family does not need the burden of this to haunt them. I hope you understand."

"Of course I do," Aunt Sherry assured her. "I wouldn't dream of hurting innocent people."

The smile that blossomed on Clarissa's face filled Debbie with joy.

They had found Aunt Sherry's birth mother, and it had turned out better than anyone could have hoped or imagined.

CHAPTER TWENTY

ebbie was still smiling on Saturday afternoon when she saw Greg and his boys walking into the depot lobby to help decorate for the dance. She, Janet, and Aunt Sherry had stayed in Newark through supper and spent hours talking with Clarissa and Katharine. They had gotten along as if they were all old friends, sharing both the highs and lows of their lives. It had been a refreshing, life-giving evening for all of them, but especially for Aunt Sherry and Clarissa.

Now, as the busyness of Saturday's activities loomed ahead, Debbie had to deliberately shift her thoughts away from Aunt Sherry and Clarissa and focus on the tasks ahead of her.

"Hello," Debbie said to Greg, Jaxon, and Julian as they walked up to her. "You're the first volunteers to arrive, which means you get to choose what job you want."

"I'll be the taste tester," Julian said with a grin.

Debbie returned his smile. "I'm not sure if that's a job today, but if it is, I'll keep you in mind. I'm sure Janet can find you a treat, if you need a little pick-me-up before getting started. She's in the café."

The boys were off and running before Debbie even finished her sentence.

Greg chuckled and then turned his attention to Debbie. "How are you?"

"I'm good—and eager to tell you what happened with my aunt Sherry." She told him about locating Clarissa and discovering the details of Aunt Sherry's birth. Clarissa had asked that the news not be shared widely, since she didn't want any negative publicity that might impact Aunt Sherry, but she had given them permission to share with their close friends and family. Since Greg already knew about the investigation, Debbie wanted him to know the outcome.

"That's—wow." Greg shook his head. "What an incredible story."

"I know." Debbie smiled. "I'm so happy we solved the mystery. They've already sent the DNA tests off and should have the answers early next week. I'm certain they'll be a match."

"Good job," Greg said to Debbie. "I'm proud of you for helping your aunt find the answers. She's fortunate to have you. We all are."

Debbie's cheeks grew warm. She was thankful the lobby doors opened at that moment and her parents entered. Debbie and Aunt Sherry had stopped by their house soon after returning from Newark to share the news with them, and they had taken it in stride. Dad was still a little reluctant to talk about the situation. He was still upset that his parents had never told them the truth, but Debbie was proud of him for putting that aside for his sister.

Soon, other volunteers arrived and began decorating the lobby with much laughter and visiting.

For the rest of the afternoon, Debbie spent most of her time directing volunteers, making decisions, and fielding questions about the event. The lobby was festive with red, white, and blue bunting, streamers, and stars. The tables were covered with red, white, and blue tablecloths, and beautiful flower centerpieces with sparkling stars were set on each one.

In the kitchen, Janet managed the volunteers who worked on the canteen dinner, and they were finished in record time. The smell of coffee permeated the air, and stacks of sandwiches, wrapped in wax paper, filled the refrigerators. Cookies, donuts, and cake sat in the bakery cabinet, and fresh fruit filled large bowls. There would also be chips and punch, though those wouldn't have necessarily been available during the canteen days. It wasn't a fancy dinner, but it would be memorable and appropriate for a canteen-style fundraiser.

Before long, the band arrived, and Debbie and Greg helped them set up in the corner of the lobby.

When everything was ready, Debbie went into the restroom to change. She had chosen a dress that reminded her of the 1940s. It was navy blue and buttoned down the front. It had a collar and a belt, and the short sleeves were cuffed. She rolled her hair at the sides and gathered it in back with a barrette. She added red lipstick and mascara and smiled at her reflection in the mirror.

"You look perfect," Mom said a few minutes later when Debbie met up with her in the lobby. "I love that dress."

"Thank you." Debbie was still smiling when Aunt Sherry arrived a little later. She was also dressed up for the occasion, as were the others who were arriving.

"Look at you," Aunt Sherry said as she hugged Debbie. "The perfect hostess."

"There's someone I'd like you to meet," Debbie said.

"Oh?"

"Harry Franklin." Debbie had seen him on the other side of the room when she exited the restroom. He stood with Patricia, near the refreshment table.

"Harry?" Aunt Sherry glanced around the room. "He was the one who found me, right?"

"Yes."

Aunt Sherry's face softened, and she nodded. "I'd love to meet him."

Debbie led her aunt across the crowded room toward Harry. The band played soft music as people trickled into the lobby. Two volunteers were at the doors, taking tickets and directing guests to the refreshment table. Debbie knew many of them, but some were strangers. Everyone was dressed up for the occasion, with several of them in 1940s-era clothing.

Harry held a cup of coffee and a donut. His laughter was rich and joyful as he shared a story with his granddaughter. When he saw Debbie approaching, his eyes shone.

"Thank you for this special treat, Debbie. I feel like I'm back in 1944 at one of the canteen dances." He shook his head. "I feel like a young man again—and I thought that was impossible."

Debbie laid her hand on Harry's forearm. "I'm happy that you're having a good time. Kim said this afternoon that this might become an annual event—so you might need to dust off your dancing shoes again next year." She glanced at Aunt Sherry. "I have someone I'd like you to meet."

Harry set his coffee and donut on the table and wiped his hands. He smiled at Sherry.

"Harry Franklin," Debbie said, "this is my aunt, Sherry Hoffman."

"Hi, Sherry." Harry extended his hand to her.

She shook his hand.

"Sherry is the baby you found on the platform in 1944," Debbie continued.

Harry's hand stilled, and he stared at Aunt Sherry. He looked confused and then incredulous.

"You're the baby?" he asked.

Aunt Sherry nodded, tears in her eyes. "Thank you, Mr. Franklin, for saving my life."

Harry shook his head. "How—when—how did you—?"

Debbie and Aunt Sherry chuckled as Harry finally let Aunt Sherry's hand go.

"It's a long story," Debbie said, "but it started a few weeks ago when Aunt Sherry found a crate in her garage."

"That's right." Harry's joyful laughter filled the room. "Miss Sherry, will you join me for some coffee and donuts? I'd love to hear all about this."

"And I'd love to tell you."

"I'll leave you two to it," Debbie said.

"You go on," Harry told her. "I'm sure you have a lot to do. Sherry and I will make ourselves comfortable and get to know one another."

Debbie's cheeks hurt from smiling as she left them and began to greet the guests. The band played Nat King Cole's classic "For Sentimental Reasons," and the lyrics, which spoke of love and promising to never be apart, echoed in Debbie's mind and heart.

Someone tapped her shoulder and said, "May I have this dance?"

Debbie turned and found Greg standing there. He had changed into a black suit. He looked handsome, and his dimples winked as he grinned at her.

"No one else is dancing yet," she protested, returning his smile.

"Someone has to start." He held out his hand. "And when a woman looks as pretty as you do in that dress, it's a shame not to let everyone admire her."

Debbie's cheeks were on fire as she placed her hand in his and let him lead her to the dance floor.

The song was gentle and nostalgic, perfect for slow dancing.

Greg faced Debbie, admiration on his face as he put his arm around her waist and drew her close.

She put her left hand on his shoulder, and their feet began to move as if they'd been dancing together for years. Even though there were no other dancers on the floor, it didn't matter.

"Thank you," Greg said. "For everything."

"You're welcome."

As the band continued to play, Debbie lost herself in the music, in the joy, and in Greg's arms.

"It's here!" Aunt Sherry announced a few days later when she came into the café. Debbie and Janet were standing behind the counter, recounting the success of the Homes for Humanity's fundraiser dance.

"What's here?" Debbie asked. She set her coffee cup down and gave her full attention to her aunt.

"The email with the results of the DNA test." Aunt Sherry's hands shook as she set her purse and phone on the counter.

Debbie leaned forward. "Have you opened it yet?"

"No." Aunt Sherry looked at her phone. "The second I got it, I jumped in the car and came here."

There were two tables of customers, but they were both toward the back of the café and didn't seem interested in the conversation near the counter.

"Do you want to be with Clarissa when you look?" Janet asked Aunt Sherry.

"No. I told her we could both open the emails on our own, and then, depending on the results, we could meet and discuss how to move forward."

Debbie put her hands on the counter for support. She watched her aunt, hopeful yet apprehensive. The results of the test could change her life in so many ways. "I'm so glad you came to share this with us."

"Well," Aunt Sherry said, taking a deep breath, "here goes."

She opened the email. After a couple of seconds, she set her phone down and looked up at Debbie.

"It's a positive match," she whispered. "Clarissa is my birth mother. I'm Baby Sarah."

Debbie came around the counter and embraced her aunt. They had been on this journey together, and having a definitive answer was such a relief.

"I'm so happy you know for sure," Debbie said as she wiped tears from her eyes. The news was bittersweet. She was disappointed that her grandparents had kept the truth from their family, but she was thankful that God had allowed it to come out in the open before it was too late for Aunt Sherry and Clarissa to meet and get to know one another.

"My kids are coming this afternoon to take me to Newark," Aunt Sherry said as she accepted a tissue from Janet and wiped her face. "They're eager to meet Clarissa and Katharine. And now, since we know for sure that I'm her daughter, it will be a very important meeting. There are a lot of things to consider, like the move I planned to make. I don't know how long I'll have with Clarissa, so I'm trying to decide if it's the best time for that."

"I'll pray you have clarity to make the best decisions," Debbie said.

"And Clarissa still wants to include all of us in her will," Aunt Sherry continued. "I was hesitant until our results came back, but now..."

"You're okay with it?"

"I don't want anything," Aunt Sherry said. "But I'm happy that my children and grandchildren will benefit from this connection." She shook her head. "It isn't about the money."

"Of course it isn't," Debbie said.

"It's about the truth coming out. It's about being honest, even when it's painful, and making wrong things right. That's what all of this is about to me."

"And," Debbie said, "it's about family. No matter how we're connected, it all comes down to family."

Aunt Sherry put her hand on Debbie's arm. "And, when it comes to family, I'm blessed beyond measure."

Debbie placed her hand over Aunt Sherry's and gave it a gentle squeeze. She couldn't have said it better. Not only was she blessed with family, but with a purposeful life and a community she loved.

It didn't get any better than that.

Dear Reader,

It was a pleasure to return to Dennison, Ohio, and the depot where this story takes place. I fell in love with these characters in the first book of the series, *Under the Apple Tree*, and have been looking forward to catching up with them again. I have especially enjoyed getting to know Eileen, Ray, and Harry, who were part of the Greatest Generation. My grandfather, Leo Gosiak, fought in Germany during WWII, but he passed away in 1983 when I was very young. I didn't know him and only have information about him from others.

In a small way, writing the stories set in the Dennison depot about people who lived during the war has made me feel closer to my grandfather. I can almost see him with the other service members coming in on the troop trains, grabbing a sandwich and a hot cup of coffee from the canteen workers. I can picture his smiling face, hear him telling a joke, and imagine both his excitement and trepidation about going overseas to serve his country. I'm not sure if he went through the Dennison depot, but it's fun to picture him there—if only for twenty minutes.

Thank you for visiting the Whistle Stop Café with me. I hope you enjoyed this story as much as I did. I look forward to seeing you here again soon.

Sincerely,
Gabrielle Meyer

ABOUT the AUTHOR

*G*abrielle Meyer lives in central Minnesota on the banks of the upper Mississippi River with her husband and four teenage children. As an employee of the Minnesota Historical Society, she fell in love with the rich history of her state and enjoys writing fictional stories inspired by real people, places, and events. Gabrielle has over thirty novels in print, including best-selling historical, contemporary, and cozy mysteries.

A GLIMPSE of the PAST

I n *For Sentimental Reasons*, we learn that Abigail Cobb met a young man who was being shipped out for military service. They only had forty-eight hours together and didn't have the opportunity to get married. This wasn't the case for everyone. During WWII, elopements and quick weddings were a common practice. In 1942 alone, there were 1.8 million weddings—up 83% from ten years before. It's estimated that two-thirds of these brides married newly enlisted soldiers.

Weddings were often thrown together quickly, with no time or money for a major affair. It was common to borrow someone else's wedding gown, raid flower gardens for bouquets, and pull together friends' and neighbors' rationed flour and sugar to make a small wedding cake.

One church in New York City, the Church of the Transfiguration on East 29th Street, between Madison and Fifth Avenues, was so popular, couples would line up to wait for their turn. The church's pastor, the Rev. Dr. Randolph Ray, said that a "quick midweek schedule" would be three ceremonies in the morning and three in the afternoon. There were over two thousand weddings there in 1942 and 1943.

By 1944, Dr. Ray was very concerned about couples marrying in this manner. He wrote a book called, *Marriage Is a Serious Business* and warned, "The hasty marriage, caused by glamour and excitement rather than by genuine affection, is one of the evil products of war."

Is it any wonder that the highest divorce rate in the 1940s was in 1946, one year after WWII ended?

No matter how or why people chose to marry during WWII, it's an interesting part of the culture of the war years, and many couples went on to live long and happy lives together.

FROM the HOME-FRONT KITCHEN

Debbie's Four-Hour Beef Stew

Ingredients:

2 lbs. stew meat

3 or 4 potatoes, peeled and
   cubed

5 or 6 carrots, peeled and sliced

2 onions, sliced

2 stalks celery, diced

2½ cups tomato juice

2 teaspoons sugar

2 teaspoons dry tapioca

Salt and pepper, to taste

2 tablespoons Lipton Onion
   Soup Mix

Directions:

1. Combine first 9 ingredients in baking dish.
2. Sprinkle soup mix on top.
3. Cover and bake at 325 degrees for 4 to 5 hours.

*Read on for a sneak peek of another exciting book
in the Whistle Stop Café Mysteries series!*

THAT'S MY BABY

BY RUTH LOGAN HERNE

"I don't like quiet days." Janet Shaw made the pronouncement as she refilled the refrigerated pastry case with slices of homemade pie Monday afternoon. Chocolate cream. Mississippi Mud. And in honor of the coming spring, fresh, spritely lemon meringue.

"For the shortest month, February sure seemed long," agreed Debbie Albright, her business partner and lifelong best friend. "But I figured spring was in the air when my buddy came to work wearing nothing but a T-shirt and jeans. A choice she's probably regretting now that the outdoor temps have nose-dived back into the thirties. It's only the beginning of March, Janet," she teased, smiling. "That's over-the-moon optimistic, even for you."

"An admittedly bad choice." Janet slanted a wry look toward the darkening sky. "Ian dropped me off here while my car's getting new tires, and I let the warm morning sweep me away."

Thick clouds hadn't just moved into the area. They'd piled in, dark and ominous, ready to deliver snow or rain, depending on the temperature. Precocious weather was simply part of their late-winter reality in Dennison, Ohio. While some stalwart crocuses peeked along walkways, nothing else of import dared blossom, despite the warmer temps they'd enjoyed that morning. With temps in the midthirties now, Janet should have brought a jacket to work. A warm one at that.

"You'd think I'd know better after nearly forty-four years of living here," she groused as Debbie finished cleaning the grill.

"I can give you a lift home, unless you'd rather walk." Debbie gave Janet a wry look. "It's not exactly T-shirt weather now, especially one sporting a full array of spring flowers." She washed her hands and dried them at the sink. "Are you just about—?"

She stopped talking as the back door flew open.

Sadie Flaherty, their childhood friend, stood framed in the doorway. Sadie owned That's My Baby, a doll store that she called "the doll hospital" over in Uhrichsville.

Sadie clutched a quilted bag to her chest. The bag was pretty, done in bright pastels. Obviously, Janet wasn't the only person wishfully thinking spring. Sadie rushed in, clearly distraught, and pushed the door shut behind her.

Janet took a step forward. "Sadie, what's wrong?"

"Can I talk to you?" Sadie whispered the request then jerked her head around as if to make sure they were alone. "Both of you?"

"Of course." Debbie motioned toward the nearest table. "What's happened? Are the kids all right? Is it Drew?"

Sadie Harper Stone had married Drew Flaherty nearly twenty years ago. It had taken them a long time to have kids, and when it finally happened, they were delighted to find out they were having twins. Both girls were avid soccer players and violinists, on the go all the time.

Janet drew out a chair for Sadie, and then she and Debbie sat down.

Sadie sank into the seat and glanced around again.

"No one's here but us," Janet assured her.

"I was checking the windows," she said. "In case anyone followed me."

"Why would anyone follow you?" Debbie frowned, clearly concerned.

"*Is* there someone following you?" pressed Janet. "I can call Ian. He'd be here in a heartbeat."

Sadie's worried expression deepened. She shook her head. "No, but they could be, and I can't believe I made such a rookie mistake." Her hands shook, and her breath came quickly. "I know better. I'm not a kid on the internet for the first time. But who'd have thought posting a picture of an old rag doll would create an issue? Not me, certainly, and yet…" She sighed, stuck her hand into the bag on her lap, and then withdrew it slowly. She clutched an old-fashioned rag doll, rudimentary in appearance. Simple rags, tied together to form a semblance of head, body, and limbs, the kind a child might have had on the prairie or during the Great Depression.

"It's this," she told them. She set the rag doll on the table. It didn't look dirty, but it did smell a little musty. "I found this as I was clearing out Aunt Lena's attic a few days ago. It was in an old trunk."

"It doesn't seem to be anything special," Debbie said. She picked up the doll and looked it over. "Probably stuffed away a long time, from the smell of it," she added.

"That's what I thought," said Sadie. "So I snapped a picture of it and posted it to my website. My followers love to see original creations like this. Depression-era handmade dolls are a good reminder to be grateful for better times."

"I don't see the problem," said Debbie. "Nothing a gentle washing and spritzing of odor-killing spray wouldn't cure."

"Except there's this." Sadie hesitated then opened her other hand. On her palm lay a tiny satin bag. It was an old-fashioned royal-blue satin with nothing polyester about it. When she upended the miniature satchel and shook it, a small brooch with a square green stone fell onto her palm. "Here's the problem," she said.

Eyes wide, Janet bent closer. "Is that a real emerald?"

"It's gorgeous," breathed Debbie. She whistled softly as she picked up the brooch for a closer look. "Truly stunning."

"Where did it come from?" asked Janet.

"Her." Sadie touched the doll. "I posted her online and got a fair number of likes and comments, but then this morning there was an email in the store's account. Here's what it said." She handed them her phone.

I am tired of secrets. So tired. I was forced to keep them for so long because of your great-grandmother, but she is long since gone, and the time for secrets is past. No more, Sadie. I will keep them no more.

That doll had a purpose. A quiet purpose, and there you are, flaunting her on social media, as if she were any old thing.

She's not. Within her folds she held potential. Freedom. Opportunity. And yet we were sworn to silence like we'd done something wrong.

I'm done.

I will no longer be quiet. At long last, I will let the truth be known. Truth about your family, your ancestors, your children, and mine.

It will alter things. There's nothing to be done about that. Lives will change.

They must.

But that is not my worry. Seeing her here, on your site, was the message I needed.

I will come. Some way, somehow, I will come. And I promise you this: The truth will set us free, as it should have long ago.

M.E.

Janet's jaw dropped. "You know this person?"

"No."

"But that line—" Janet pointed to the message. "'Within her folds she held potential. Freedom. Opportunity.' Does that mean this person knew something was hidden inside a doll that's probably at least fifty years old?"

"Older than that," Sadie said. "I think the doll dates back to World War II. My great-aunt Lena had Gee Gee living with her after Great-Grandpa passed away. Gee Gee was my great-grandmother, Annie Harper. Most of Gee Gee's stuff got moved to Aunt Lena's attic along with the tons of things already up there. There were newspapers in the chest," she continued. "For packing, I think. To cushion things. They were dated 1950."

"Where were they from?" Janet asked.

"New York City," Sadie said. She paused and took a breath. "Finding the doll and the brooch was weird, but that's not what has me upset. My family had secrets."

She lifted a napkin from the miniature rack on the table and twisted it between her fingers. "I've known that for a long time. I don't know what they are, but I know they exist," she continued. "There were whispers and dark looks between the adults when I was small, and sometimes Gee Gee would get this strange expression on her face. Not just scared. Terrified, as if someone was after her. Aunt Lena called it the 'demons of war,' but there was no explanation about what she meant by that."

She took a deep breath. "We weren't allowed to talk about World War II, or the emigration, or even do family research because Gee Gee was so sensitive to it. By the time I was old enough to demand answers, my life had gotten busy."

"I hear you," Janet said. "Jobs, kids, life. It piles on."

"But now Aunt Lena's gone, I've inherited what was her home and the business we both loved, and out of the blue comes some mysterious email." She tapped the *Do Not Reply to This Email* line on the printout. "An email talking about secrets, about the doll, about changing lives. It creeped me out."

Sadie sighed. "I don't have anyone to ask about any of this. Dad's gone, and Mom's remarried and living in Florida with her new husband. Aunt Lena was the last one of the Harpers who would have remembered anything, and now she's gone too. I'm the one who has to worry about what this person knows about my family.

"He or she says they'll come. How am I supposed to handle that? Having a random stranger threaten to show up? And how will I even know who he or she is?"

"Did you try answering it?" asked Debbie.

"It says 'do not reply.'" Sadie met Debbie's gaze, puzzled. "So I can't answer it. Right?"

"I'd give it a try, see what you get," Debbie replied. "The 'do not reply' might just be a discouragement. Or, you could be right, and your letter might go to a vast email wasteland somewhere. Either way, it can't hurt to try, can it?"

Sadie shook her head. "You're right. I'll do that when I get home. Maybe I'll get an answer." She sighed and smiled ruefully. "I'm such a rule follower. It said 'do not reply,' so I didn't. Where has my spirit of adventure gone?"

"It's still there," Janet assured her. "It's just momentarily knocked out." She tapped a finger to the originator's email address. "It's hard to know exactly what the person is thinking from the email, but it's not hard to hear the angst. Would it be okay if Debbie and I look into this for you? See what we can find? You can let us know if your response gets a reaction."

Sadie nodded. "I was hoping you'd offer. That's why I came to you two. You've got a knack for untying knots, and I'm too close to this to do anything rational. I was just thinking this was Grandma Mary's or Gee Gee's old doll that got stuffed in an old trunk a long time ago. And I don't think I would have ever found the brooch inside without that email."

"You didn't feel it in the doll?" Janet asked.

"No," Sadie said. "I thought the hard bit was just some rubber or stone they built the doll around." She frowned. "From the little I do know, my family came here right after World War II with nothing, so where does an emerald brooch fit? Is it part of my heritage?

Hidden for safekeeping, then misplaced? Or something more sinister? What if my ancestors were part of something illegal? And who is this anonymous note writer?" She indicated the email with a glance toward her phone. "They know who I am, where my business is, and where I live. But I know nothing about them, their intentions, or how they knew something was hidden in the doll."

"Secrets have a way of working their way to the surface eventually," said Janet.

Sadie grimaced. "I don't know whether I should be comforted by that or not," she said.

"We'll look into it," Janet promised. "Quietly. There may be a perfectly innocent reason—"

"For a pricey brooch to be hidden in a tacky rag doll and some random stranger knowing about it?"

Janet laid her hand over her friend's. "No use borrowing trouble, Sadie. We'll see what we can find. In the meantime, do you want to keep the brooch in the safe at my house? I can promise it'll be secure there."

Sadie met Janet's gaze. "Yes."

"And how should she handle Mr. or Ms. Anonymous Message Sender?" mused Debbie as Janet slipped the tiny satin bag into her pocket. "This person obviously follows Sadie's social media. Are they expecting a reaction?"

"They might be expecting it, but that doesn't mean we give them the satisfaction of one," said Janet. "My advice is to ignore it. Say nothing. Continue your normal day-to-day posts."

Sadie took a deep breath. She seemed calmer already.

"I think that's good advice," said Debbie. "Do you have any old family pictures, Sadie? From World War II or before?"

Sadie thought for a moment before answering. "Mom might have had some. If she did, they'd be up in our attic. I don't think there are very many. People didn't have the money for film or developing back then, not with the war on."

"Just see what you can find," advised Janet.

"Sadie, would you like coffee?" Debbie asked. "Or hot chocolate? Anything?"

Sadie stood. "I've got to get back. The girls have their Tuesday violin lessons with Miss Rita, and they'll need a ride to her place." She clutched the quilted bag tighter to her chest. "Thank you. I didn't know where to turn, and I don't want the police involved, because if there's something unsavory about our family history, I want to know first."

"Call me if you find any pictures," said Janet as Sadie moved to the door. "We'll come over and check them out with you."

"I will." She hurried through the front door and exited through the lobby side of the building. The wind-whipped storm slapped slush-laden drops around her as she dashed to the parking lot across the street.

"You got your wish," noted Debbie as she stood. She crossed the room and flicked off the lights.

"The only thing I'm wishing is that I'd worn a coat today."

"I meant the other wish." Debbie moved toward the door. "The one about not liking quiet days. Sadie's visit took care of that, didn't it?"

Janet agreed. Sadie's request had put a whole new spin on this particular day. "It sure did. And just when I think I'm relegated to dashing to your car in this slop, a hero comes along." She smiled as Ian pulled up to the curb. And as she and Debbie hurried to their cars, the brooch in her pocket claimed her thoughts.

Whose was it?

Why was it hidden in a musty doll, then left, forgotten, in an old trunk?

And how did some anonymous person know about it?

That might be the biggest question of all.

While you are waiting for the next fascinating story in the Whistle Stop Café Mysteries, check out some other Guideposts mystery series!

SAVANNAH SECRETS

Welcome to Savannah, Georgia, a picture-perfect Southern city known for its manicured parks, moss-covered oaks, and antebellum architecture. Walk down one of the cobblestone streets, and you'll come upon Magnolia Investigations. It is here where two friends have joined forces to unravel some of Savannah's deepest secrets. Tag along as clues are exposed, red herrings discarded, and thrilling surprises revealed. Find inspiration in the special bond between Meredith Bellefontaine and Julia Foley. Cheer the friends on as they listen to their hearts and rely on their faith to solve each new case that comes their way.

The Hidden Gate
A Fallen Petal
Double Trouble
Whispering Bells
Where Time Stood Still
The Weight of Years
Willful Transgressions

WHISTLE STOP CAFÉ MYSTERIES

Season's Meetings
Southern Fried Secrets
The Greatest of These
Patterns of Deception
The Waving Girl
Beneath a Dragon Moon
Garden Variety Crimes
Meant for Good
A Bone to Pick
Honeybees & Legacies
True Grits
Sapphire Secret
Jingle Bell Heist
Buried Secrets
A Puzzle of Pearls
Facing the Facts
Resurrecting Trouble
Forever and a Day

MYSTERIES *of* MARTHA'S VINEYARD

Priscilla Latham Grant has inherited a lighthouse! So with not much more than a strong will and a sore heart, the recent widow says goodbye to her lifelong Kansas home and heads to the quaint and historic island of Martha's Vineyard, Massachusetts. There, she comes face-to-face with adventures, which include her trusty canine friend, Jake, three delightful cousins she didn't know she had, and Gerald O'Bannon, a handsome Coast Guard captain—plus head-scratching mysteries that crop up with surprising regularity.

A Light in the Darkness
Like a Fish Out of Water
Adrift
Maiden of the Mist
Making Waves
Don't Rock the Boat
A Port in the Storm
Thicker Than Water
Swept Away
Bridge Over Troubled Waters
Smoke on the Water
Shifting Sands
Shark Bait
Seascape in Shadows

Storm Tide
Water Flows Uphill
Catch of the Day
Beyond the Sea
Wider Than an Ocean
Sheeps Passing in the Night
Sail Away Home
Waves of Doubt
Lifeline
Flotsam & Jetsam
Just Over the Horizon

MIRACLES & MYSTERIES
of MERCY HOSPITAL

Four talented women from very different walks of life witness the miracles happening around them at Mercy Hospital and soon become fast friends. Join Joy Atkins, Evelyn Perry, Anne Mabry, and Shirley Bashore as, together, they solve the puzzling mysteries that arise at this Charleston, South Carolina, historic hospital—rumored to be under the protection of a guardian angel. Come along as our quartet of faithful friends solve mysteries, stumble upon a few of the hospital's hidden and forgotten passageways, and discover historical treasures along the way! This fast-paced series is filled with inspiration, adventure, mystery, delightful humor, and loads of Southern charm!

Where Mercy Begins
Prescription for Mystery
Angels Watching Over Me
A Change of Art
Conscious Decisions
Surrounded by Mercy
Broken Bonds
Mercy's Healing
To Heal a Heart

A Cross to Bear

Merciful Secrecy

Sunken Hopes

Hair Today, Gone Tomorrow

Pain Relief

Redeemed by Mercy

A Genius Solution

A Hard Pill to Swallow

Ill at Ease

'Twas the Clue Before Christmas

A NOTE FROM the EDITORS

We hope you enjoyed another exciting volume in the Whistle Stop Café Mysteries series, published by Guideposts. For over seventy-five years, Guideposts, a nonprofit organization, has been driven by a vision of a world filled with hope. We aspire to be the voice of a trusted friend, a friend who makes you feel more hopeful and connected.

By making a purchase from Guideposts, you join our community in touching millions of lives, inspiring them to believe that all things are possible through faith, hope, and prayer. Your continued support allows us to provide uplifting resources to those in need. Whether through our communities, websites, apps, or publications, we inspire our audiences, bring them together, and comfort, uplift, entertain, and guide them. Visit us at guideposts.org to learn more.

We would love to hear from you. Write us at Guideposts, P.O. Box 5815, Harlan, Iowa 51593 or call us at (800) 932-2145. Did you love *For Sentimental Reasons*? Leave a review for this product on guideposts.org/shop. Your feedback helps others in our community find relevant products.

Find inspiration, find faith, find Guideposts.

Shop our best sellers and favorites at
guideposts.org/shop

Or scan the QR code to go directly to our Shop

Find more inspiring stories in these best-loved Guideposts fiction series!

Mysteries of Lancaster County

Follow the Classen sisters as they unravel clues and uncover hidden secrets in Mysteries of Lancaster County. As you get to know these women and their friends, you'll see how God brings each of them together for a fresh start in life.

Secrets of Wayfarers Inn

Retired schoolteachers find themselves owners of an old warehouse-turned-inn that is filled with hidden passages, buried secrets, and stunning surprises that will set them on a course to puzzling mysteries from the Underground Railroad.

Tearoom Mysteries Series

Mix one stately Victorian home, a charming lakeside town in Maine, and two adventurous cousins with a passion for tea and hospitality. Add a large scoop of intriguing mystery, and sprinkle generously with faith, family, and friends, and you have the recipe for *Tearoom Mysteries*.

Ordinary Women of the Bible

Richly imagined stories—based on facts from the Bible—have all the plot twists and suspense of a great mystery, while bringing you fascinating insights on what it was like to be a woman living in the ancient world.

To learn more about these books, visit Guideposts.org/Shop